My Mistress Whispers and Roars

Published in the United States by Wooden Fish Publications
Bolinas, California

My Mistress Whispers and Roars
Griff Marshall
ISBN #: 978-1-365-47304-3
Manufactured in the United States of America
9 8 7 6 5 4 3 2
FIRST EDITION
Back cover photo: Austin Montreil Leonard
Cover photo: Griff Marshall

Wooden Fish Publications
Post Office Box 420
Bolinas, California 94924

Bob,
Glad to have spent
a day with you

My Mistress Whispers and Roars

by Griff Marshall

And the boys

All The Best

Griff

Table of Contents

This Book is humbly, sincerely and gratefully dedicated to my wife, my best friend and soul mate, Michelie, and to the family we are raising here in Bend, Oregon. And also to those who have crossed this angler's path over the past thirty years.

Introduction

The "Others"

Winter 2016

I'm married. Happily so. No really, I am. For the second time. So incredibly happily married. For real. Now I know what you're thinking, *the more someone tries to buttress a statement, the less believable it is.* But in my case, I really am, truthfully, deeply happy to be married to my wife. And it's been a long time since I've known any other life. A while. Like a really, very long time. I'm on my second wife now. My first, Theresa, like her namesake, is a saint. She's known me for more than half my life. While we were married she was a great friend and partner. Still is. We raised my favorite human, Jasper, together. Our lives saw baffling changes over the years we were together, apart, back together and, ultimately, apart but perhaps more together than ever, if that makes any sense. We went from starving artists living under a slumlord's roof in San Francisco, to successful business people living north in Marin County. We owned a home and business. We were close with countless family and friends. We had a dog. I think now as we -you and I that is- retrace this time, it's fair to say that Theresa and I lived an enviable life; our nearest and dearest saw us as a shining example of the complete young family. And perhaps we were.

But you see, there was this thing. This problem afflicted me. It wasn't entirely veiled from the world. But the part of it seen by friends and family was quite simply the tip of a very large, potentially very destructive iceberg. The problem was that there were, you know, *others.* Lots of them actually. They had been there before I met

Theresa, hadn't left, and I couldn't make them go away. Much as the realities of my life dictated that I should find distractions, like golf or mountain biking, I just couldn't turn and go. These mistresses - commonly referred to as the "*others*" or "*other ones*"- were a force in my life. They haunted my dreams, kept me company in traffic jams, occupied my psyche during airplane rides. They never directly intruded, instead staying a safe distance, but all the while calling to me, beckoning as sirens might, a series of lighthouses with their seductive, hypnotically rotating lights, leading me not to some safe harbor but, instead, into their canyon-deep, utterly engulfing embrace. Were I a man of sterner resoluteness I would have walked away from these indiscretions. I would have put family first, been a more loyal husband, a singularly devoted dad and wrestled free the savage-strong grip. But you see, I was -and am- not a man of such temerity. No, after all these decades, I have to live with the reality that I am a creep, a derelict, a self-serving hypocritical asshole.

But it's not my fault. It's theirs. The *others*.

Just like a man unable to control his greater impulses after injecting his first syringe full of heroin, I have been put under a spell, a decision-warping lust. Granted, my overpowering, all-consuming needs most likely won't lead to that tragic end my oldest brother suffered at the diabolical hand of drugs. But they can take on an unhealthy hunger. And while there are trained professionals with industrial-strength prescription medications at their disposal to cure me, I have shunned any meaningful recovery. In light of everything that's been ruined, the feelings hurt, the abandoned responsibilities, the betrayed relationships, I'm still under their spell. The only solace I find in these quiet moments, when no one else is around, when it's just me, a half-drunk cup of coffee and my sleeping dog, is that I never meant to hurt anyone. I don't think I'm a bad person at my core, just a wayward soul held in the insatiable grip of an especially beautiful, seductive and generous infatuation.

My addiction has intermittently loosened and tightened its hold over all these years, but never remotely released me. There are days when I feel a modicum of self-restraint. There are weeks and months that pass without significant relapse. But the *need* is always there. *They,* those romantic, wretched *others,* are always there. Some are far enough away now that the simple physical distance acts as a functioning barrier. But others, oh those wanton coquettes, are near enough that I could sneak in a mid-afternoon quickie and barely be missed. It is a dangerous proximity. And so instead of visiting one of them, I often lock myself here, in this chaotic mess of a den and write. Occasionally, these respites are enough; I'll emerge almost having forgotten the pull. Every now and again I re-engage the world with a renewed resolve that I can kick it. I'll convince myself that thirty-plus years of a certain proclivity does not an unbreakable habit make; I can evaluate all the cost/risk analysis and rationalize my way back to a social normalcy; the potential that loved ones see in me might still be realized. But then I hear the *others'* call. It might be a whisper in the wind while walking the dog, or a rustling of pine needles overhead on a bike ride. It might even be the passing of a cloud when playing with my young daughter at the park. Or, it might occur in that semi-panicked, wide-eyed moment when last night becomes today. But when it comes, it comes. And it doesn't go away. It's not exactly the moth to the flame thing, but it *is* an unavoidable attraction with obvious detriment. And if I don't respond right away, the nagging will become unrelenting. My dreams will be intruded by the *others*. The last thing I think about before sleep, the first image that arrives when I wake, they are terrier-tenacious and heron-unwavering. And so I go to them. It's just what I do.

So you know, there has been no one "type" for me. As my addiction blossomed and my need for a fix caused worse and worse errors in judgment, I found myself travelling, often great distances and at great expense, to be with the *others*. I was indiscriminate. If one of them would have me, I was in. Maybe for one quick day and night, or sometimes extended visits during which I'd ply their every crevice in search of answers, attempting to learn their intricacies; I'd give everything I had hoping that they would in turn give up pieces of themself. And increasingly, I realized that the more distinction there was from one *other* to the next challenged me to adapt and evolve. I didn't just go for the big-boned brawlers, nor for that matter the small, gentle ones. They might be loud and rambunctious, perfectly willing and able to break me in two. They might be the silent type, moving slowly through life, in no obvious rush but getting to their destination with or without me. We might bore of each other in a matter of hours, or the affair might take on a life of its own, demanding huge sacrifices, offering unheard of rewards, a delirium unknown before their embrace. The more fierce the affliction, the less the details seemed to matter.

And now my second wife, Michelie and our daughter Lola, are the unwitting victims of my malaise. Michelie *sort* of knew what she was getting into. Lola, on the other hand, is the most pure, innocent creature. She in no way deserves the life she's been born into and the one that lay ahead. A child should possess an inalienable right to her parent's -both of them- being there for her; not running off to serve a selfish need. Already, at just five-years old, countless mornings she's arisen to find me gone, off with some *other* or another. I come home, sweat stained, filthy, smelling vaguely of fish and exhausted. She tries to act happy to see me but somewhere in her untarnished view of the world she has to know where I've been and what I was doing. Her angelic, smiling understanding makes me want to weep with self-loathing.

Back in California, for a while there, I almost felt cured. The *others* had retreated a little. The combination of lack of time, money and desire conspired to alleviate some of my afflictions acuteness. It was a welcome respite. My son was finishing high school. Michelie and I were welcoming our daughter into the world. I was basically unemployed, living amongst the most wretched congregation of horrifically aspirational assholes perhaps ever assembled in one county, trying to keep my son's head screwed on straight as he navigated high school. And for one brief era of my "grown" life, the *others* retreated, almost as if they had a heart after all. Those few years were not filled with light for me. I was trudging. So was everyone around me. Can you imagine a place where the average income surpasses any concept of "average" and yet the vast majority of people are trudging? You probably can. It is a hideous environment; a contaminated, toxic social cesspool. And we were stuck there. Trudging. Man, I like that word. Every now and again there is a word that just hits the nail on the head so squarely. This is one of those times.

So for a while the *others* seemed to have an almost sympathetic absence from my life. Months would pass with barely a blip. Oh, I thought about them. Don't get the wrong idea here. I *wanted* them. But the urge, that pulse-heightening need, was largely nonexistent.

Then Jasper graduated high school. And we moved. To Oregon. Maybe a fresh start in a new place, far from the *others* I'd grown accustomed to would shelter me. Wrong.

Here in Oregon the weather is different. The terrain is new. The community entirely fresh. But there is no change in me. The spell is wickedly mighty. The *others* keep coming, long after you'd think a man of my age would be of any interest. It would appear that I cannot run from this disease and those who feed it. Just please know and believe, dear reader, that I do feel remorse and shame; I do wish I'd been made of more willpower, been a better father, son, brother, husband and friend.

You know, it just occurred to me that some might misinterpret this bit of confessional writing and assume that I've been caddish with other women. But no, the *others* of which I write, the temptresses that have haunted more breaths than left alone, are rivers. The silky smooth, ever-changing, all-consuming addiction I have is to rivers *and* their denizens.

Oh, to be a metaphor.

I'm a fly-fishing addict. But it's not just the fish I'm addicted to; it's where they live. I believe it was Gierach who wrote, "Trout do not live in ugly places." Very early on, while living in the dingiest apartment I could find in San Francisco, aspiring to be poet and philosopher, Charles Bukowski -such was my degree of self-contempt and loathing, but more on that later- I learned that Gierach was right. Every time I went to explore a thin blue ribbon descending the Sierra I found another beautiful, vibrant, challenging embrace. Another mistress. Another seduction away from all the responsibilities a young man should take a wee more seriously. One after another they appeared, beckoning, with an unquenchable thirst for my attention. And, as I mentioned earlier, they would not be denied.

Now here I am in Oregon, literally surrounded by willing *others*, and maybe it's that I've just gotten used to it, or maybe old age and low testosterone are beginning to provide balance. Perhaps those closest to me have just amended their expectations of my capabilities and are therefore less stressed out over my lack of, well, lack of anything substantial. But for some reason, here and now, the *others* and I seem to have found some balance. I guess that's why I've made this awkward confession. And maybe it's why I can write what I'm about to write. It is now time to uncloak this hidden cache of seductresses. To achieve any meaningful catharsis, I must retrace each misconceived step; honor and give due respect these sinister angels and pay homage those who have touched me the deepest. I'm compelled to go back to the very first one, and trace lightly with feather-soft fingertips the landscape of this journey right up until now.

These are stories about the mistresses in my life for the last thirty years. And how they whisper and roar.

Into the night.
Through the valley.
Over the mountain.
Into her canyon.
She awaits.

Chapter 1

The Early Crushes

Not long after discovering fly fishing, having come from a lifetime of drowning bait to catch dinner in San Francisco Bay and lure fishing for trout in nearby lakes, I made a series of solo trips up to the Sierra Nevada mountain range. These were the initial forays into fishing rivers and streams with a fly rod. After a year or so of learning to cast and tie knots -with the occasional trout thrown in- on a local lake, my attention was drawn eastward. These trips were also an attempt to endear myself to a new love. But first, a bit of preamble.

I was at the time, it should be known, a heartbroken, miserable wreck. A real, flesh and bones woman had seen to it to destroy all I held dear; to decimate any reason for hope in the future; to bold-facedly remove any good I may have had in my soul and torch it in the most inhumane and humiliating fashion. Yea, I got dumped. But it was way, far worse than that. This was THE ONE, she of sublime beauty, stunning intellect, razor-sharp wit, an unflinchingly caring heart. I'd invested everything in us. Even at the tender age of twenty-one, I would have bet the farm that we'd marry, have and live in a cabin tucked away in a Fairfax redwood grove, me becoming a rock star, her a teacher of disabled children. This destiny was fixed in my vision just as my bulbous nose is on my face. Then, one day, leaving a question mark so indelible it lingers today, thirty years on, she flicked a switch and stopped loving me. Told me so straight to my face one night outside the café where I worked in the then quaint town of Mill Valley. Just didn't love me anymore. No real explanation. Not that one was needed. The heart says what it says and does what it does. And I *was* an asshole; a self-serving degenerate.

But she KNEW THAT going in. And I was under some misguided impression that to become a rock star one needed to possess those "qualities". Anyway, I loved her more than life itself, professed so as might a child with Tourette's. Loved her the best I knew how. And she loved me, of that I'm certain. Until she stopped.

The rest of that sordid tale will be chronicled in a novel I'll finish writing someday, and -spoiler alert- it doesn't end well. One of us survives, that much I'll disclose here and now. But what did occur in the turbulent wake, the drunken, debaucherous, self-loathing-fueled haze after she left, is that I discovered fly fishing. Then the clouds parted, angels sang, my soul was rediscovered, a new keel was affixed my spirit and I began to weep less often.

It was in this state that I ventured east, far from the fog-shrouded hill in San Francisco where I'd taken the shittiest apartment I could find. Oh, I could have afforded something much nicer, even on my meager earnings. It was, after all 1985 and places were cheap. But I was convinced that I needed to live amongst the rats, the rotten, festering garbage. I was up to my eyeballs in a Bukowskian underworld, where hope is lost but for the salvation of one's essence through the demeaning of one's body; that tearing apart the mortal coil would alleviate the waking nightmare; that only through words and music and expression would the ties that bound be undone. And in retrospect, I was entirely correct. So it was not from the internal, conceptual fog that I fled, but from the real, face-moistening stuff, which swept over the hill day after day, week after week, all summer long. I craved sunshine. And I craved solitude.

Both, I was convinced, could be found a few hours east in the Sierra Nevada mountain range. The great spine had entertained me endlessly as a child. Our family visited friends in Lake Tahoe throughout the seasons. I spent one winter as a ski bum up there. We camped occasionally. I'd catch a trout every now and then on a lure or salmon eggs, promptly breaking its neck and proudly removing entrails in preparation of a feast. Life was so much simpler then. Perhaps that is what I also craved in my earliest exploration thirty-plus years ago. I yearned for some solace, distraction, and an equation with fewer moving targets.

What I discovered was that I was blind, deaf and dumb. And it was in this stupor I stumbled upon a truth I'd sheltered myself from, one that my parents had neglected to explain, an element my family was utterly ignorant of, my closest friends and band mates would never comprehend. Not all of this revelation came at once. It sort of trickled in. Each adventure to the mountains was a slow drip of my awakening as a man, as a human, as a son, brother, friend, and artist. The most important personal aspect, the truth I found in myself that I don't think I'd ever known, was that I was lover, and a good one at that. This would come especially hesitatingly, through massive struggle, through months and years of turmoil, self-deprecation and failure.

First, there was stumbling, a figurative searching with arms outstretched into the darkness. I was learning how to walk again, only this time with rivers tugging at my legs the whole time. While my soul dawdled out amidst the ether in search of meaning, my body wandered amongst towering pine trees, over furnace-hot granite, under cobalt skies, one hand clutching a fly rod. And while my actual heart -the one of four valves- pulsed blood through veins as needed, the perhaps more significant, although metaphorical one, beat only sporadically, seemingly having lost the will to love completely, to adore without regard for consequence, to give of self without the need for reciprocation, to lay bare the most sensitive things with utter abandon.

Through self-inflicted CPR, allowing the flowing waters, whistling winds and blankets of stars to be my defibrillator, that heart, the one I needed as much as the one in my chest, came back to life, pumping light into the blackness consuming my soul. A great and grand new lover was born. An intent was discovered. My meaning was to encounter, romance, seduce, capture and ultimately love unconditionally the most beautiful creature ever conceived. No, I'm not talking about myself! This isn't a self-help book, for Pete's sake. No, the creature of which I speak is the finned and spotted kind. Trout. I know what you're thinking, Damn, dude, they're just fish. How romantic is that? Well A: Trout are much more than 'just fish' and B: You're an asshole for thinking that. Trout and where they live -along with massive doses of Joni Mitchell and The Smiths- saved me from complete self-annihilation. And they saved the world from some second-rate Charles Bukowski, whinging about the winsomeness of humanity's downfall. So be appreciative.

With little or no idea of what I was doing on my early explorations, I embraced my blindness. Several days at a time were spent roaming up and down the granite and pine canyon of the Silver Fork of the American River. She was my first. I was camping in an undeveloped site along the banks. Hour after hour was spent peering into the clear water, searching for some sign as to what the hell I should do. I probably had one box with a couple dozen flies. There were a few Prince Nymphs, some Bird's Nests, Wooly Buggers and Pheasant Tails for subsurface. My dry offerings consisted of Adams, Light Cahills and Royal Wulffs. My friend, Dan from the Orvis store in San Francisco had told me they were all effective on Sierra streams, but gave little input otherwise. I think he sensed that I was wanting to figure things out for myself. I knew nothing about nymph techniques, less about reading moving water. So metaphorically I was feeling my way around in near pitch-black darkness. But the lack of understanding was what I needed; I welcomed the unfamiliar into my realm. One thing I discovered on those early trips was that complete and utter focus was needed to properly attend to the art of fly fishing. All else must be tuned out. Whatever demons followed me to the river, they were vanquished while fishing. And I *was* fishing. Just not doing much *catching*. From pool to pool, through stretches of tumbling pocket water, in each bouncing riffle, I probed. Hours would pass in seeming minutes. Days would vanish. Nights were spent strumming my guitar and singing to campfire flames and unseen squirrels or silently berating the universe for inflicting my heartache; sometimes this wasn't done so silently. Then, after a few days of solitude, I would reenter the world of grey skies, grey sidewalks, grey hearts.

I'm not kidding or exaggerating when I state that more than one of these trips came and went before I caught a fish, on the fly rod, that is. Oh, I captured, killed and ate trout, but those were fooled the old-fashioned way, death by lure. Indeed, I believe it was on the third such solo trip, actually on my way home, when *the* moment occurred. There is a short accessible stretch of the Silver Fork, just above its confluence with the South Fork of the American River. Would you believe that just now, when I went to Google Maps and found that same spot, my heart skipped a beat and I remembered exactly how I felt that day? You never forget your first... It was down there, scrambling over granite boulders the size of small houses, where it happened. I was casting my first rod, a Cortland 9' 6wt 4pc "just-add-water" kit. I named that rod The Wand. On the end of my leader was a Bitch's Creek. It must have been lead-wrapped. There were no bead-head flies then. And there were no indicators either. The great black and yellow fly splashed into a swirling pool amidst coarse, sloping granite houses. I was easily eight feet above the water, which was so clear I could see currents develope and dissipate with thousands of tiny bubbles forming miniature tornadoes. With rod held out over the river I somehow produced a sufficient drift. The grab was sudden and produced a breath-stealing shock; that of a lover's initial caress, of a kiss holding promise of another. Through a haze of startled disbelief I set the hook into an invisible energy force beneath dozens of little bubble tornadoes. The rod bent, at least from the middle ferrule to the tip, and bounced absorbing headshakes from below. It occurred at some point that there was no way to get near enough the water to land the fish, which I intended to release. No sense in killing this one. I was heading back to the grey land of pizza slices and foil-wrapped burritos. Turned out the leader and knots were stout enough for me to eventually yard the fish out of the river and up to me. Much as I'd love to profess my delicate handling and loving release, the truth is far more sordid. My hands were not wet. I'm quite sure I squeezed far too tightly and kept it out of the water too long. Its plunge back down to the river was inelegant. But before letting the fish go I held it and admired every aspect. I'd learn later that it was a wild fish, as no hatchery trout were stocked in that area. It had hundreds of epic, multi-sized spots covering every parts of its body, save the pure white belly. Even its reddish-green fins were patterned with tiny spots. Its beauty swam frantically in my psyche in the moments after it swam to freedom. Heart welled from chest. Spirit soared into towering cumulous. Soul and body collided. And my life had purpose again.

Think back now, perhaps with eyes closed, to a time you had such an experience. A moment when a new and vivid clarity came over you. A time of true, undeniable revelation. A seminal event that still shapes your every waking breath. It may have been when you first made eye contact with the love of your life. Or how it felt to cradle your first child, minutes after it entered the world. It could be when you found God, or God found you, or a meeting with some other entity you've since learned to worship with your every fiber. Go there now. See if you can. There was scent, a tactile sensation, a whispering wind, an echoing church or mosque, a piercing element that still languishes within you today. Find it and you'll understand what that trout meant to me.

That moment was the beginning of an ongoing courtship with the Silver Fork. She was convenient, beautiful, welcoming and generous. I was still fumbling and lacking confidence of purpose. Often I'd visit for less than twenty-four hours. Her canyon would welcome me in the middle of the night and I'd be back in San Francisco the next night for band practice or a gig. Some trips would last days. I'd just disappear from everything and everybody and go fishing. It was my emergence as a loner, an aspiring monk armed with not a Shaolin, but a flimsy wand meant to cast away evil, meant to allow me precious minutes of respite from heartbreak, disenchantment and the noise of a city. I was slowly discovering where I was supposed to be, not where I was expected. It was an awakening of epic and damning proportions. And it was the true birth of a fly-fishing addict.

A year would pass before the next *other* entered my life. The encounter with this one actually occurred after several failed "first dates" with other *others*. Orvis Dan had tried valiantly to set me up. I think he knew that as fun and generous a mistress as the Silver Fork had become, as a man and aspiring angler, I needed more diversity. He insisted I not settle. The prodding was relentless enough for me to turn my back on my first crush. And so to Trout Country I ventured; the storied, legendary canyons of the McCloud and Pitt Rivers; the crowds and insanity of Power House #2 on Hat Creek; the silent, oozing swirls of the Fall River. I went humbly, understanding that these *others* were most likely out of my league. With bowed head and hat in hand I introduced myself. Their beauty was intimidating and inspiring. It was with a boy's excitement and eagerness that I attempted engagement. And it was with a heartless alacrity I was denied any meaningful interaction. At the time I felt the rejection deeply, in a sensitive place still bruised and tender. As I sulked away, confidence shattered, courage leveled, there was a loneliness I'd never known. Even back when I "lived" on a remote beach in the Virgin Islands, literally not seeing another soul for days on end, I hadn't felt so lonely. Perhaps because then I knew what I was getting into. On my initial forays into the Silver Fork, it was the same. And in those places I went for the lack of interaction with people, a dearth of anything resembling social behavior. But on the very first lap of Trout County, I went feeling sure there would be another *other* for me to embrace, and to in turn reward me my attraction. But there was no reciprocation. I was ready to love. But just as a woman in a bar might do —and, let's face it, has done- the abjuration was swift, conclusive and transmitted to the depths of my soul. A scar was left.

On the drive home, with a couple days before I was expected anywhere, I drove south from Burney through Lassen National Park. State highway 89, for those of you unfamiliar, pretty much traces a line along the Sierra from the town of Mt Shasta at the north, all the way passed Lake Tahoe, ending at highway 395 near the border with Nevada. It's a magnificent drive if you're ever looking for one. Small towns come and go, but for the most part the road traverses the spine, following rivers and streams, around lakes, with ancient pine trees numerous as blades of grass in a pasture. Heading south from Lassen I diverted to a county road that appeared to go around a reservoir and then drop into a steep canyon with a river or creek etched into the bottom. That canyon would eventually deposit me on the road I'd take to get back to the great Central Valley and the highways that would lead me home. So it seemed a very low-risk detour.

In those days it was just me and a late-80's Nissan King-Cab 4x4 pickup truck. Her name was Blanca. It was a white truck. She and I had gone across the country twice, driven through almost every state, created memories good and bad. And in those early days of exploration, she was as noble a steed as there ever was. On this day, as we slowly peddled homeward, tail tucked between legs, the dog-eared Gazetteer showing a potential for some action, the decision to see what lay beyond the known was an easy one. The map showed pavement becoming dirt, winding around a large reservoir then descending quickly. The day was warm. Bob Marley sang from the door speakers. A road T'ed into 89. We turned right. It was one of those times when a seemingly innocuous decision, easily made in the moment, leads to a life-altering event.

Where the road turned to dirt, I grabbed a cold beer from the cooler. At first the rutted track was easy enough to cruise on. Then it gradually became one pothole after another, alternating sides. The reservoir was indeed a large one. But it was not a recreational lake. There were no campgrounds or boat ramps. As I bounced along, high above the waterline, I increasingly felt insignificant in the vast, uninhabited forest. It would take nearly an hour to finally get to the dam. I stopped there and got out to stretch and take a few deep breaths. As comfortable as I've always been with solo exploration, this little side trip had a pretty heavy feel to it. I was over halfway to my destination, but from the small pullout, peering down into the throat of a massive canyon, nary a road to be seen amongst the old growth forest, I initially considered backtracking. The trip to there had been rugged enough. From the looks of what lay ahead, it wasn't about to get any better. After a brief moment of self-doubt morphing into a girded resolve to continue, Blanca and I were on our way into the deep unknown.

A half hour later I was ruing the call to proceed. The road was more of a once-was jeep track as it switched back and forth down a really steep ravine. At one point it took nearly ten minutes to go a quarter mile, such was the nasty, deteriorated road. On one side was a crumbling, carved out hillside, littering big rocks into the way. The other was a near-vertical drop into the forest below. Then there would be a small clearing with a U-turn and the road went back the other direction. Several times I wondered why it was even open for public use. The small stream of water released from the reservoir above finally came in to join the road and soon I was approaching a big hydroelectric facility. This is one of many, many such structures in California. Pacific Gas and Electric (PG&E) has dammed and rerouted countless rivers throughout the state. Some of these facilities have enhanced fishing, some have ended it. I drove slowly through, the buzz of live electricity overwhelming all else. Then the road went around a small lake, the afterbay, which had an earthen dam at the far end. Here the road led away from the water for a mile or two. Then they rejoined. And that's where we met, my new *other* and I.

She was unspectacular at first, lacking overt communication skills. And I was underwhelmed, feeling a paucity of inspiration. It was not the same rushing of blood that accompanied laying eyes on the McCloud. No, this one was small, without any immediate grandeur. She lay deep in a slot canyon, no doubt having once upon a time been a seasonal spectacle with raging torrents tearing at the narrow crevice. At a small bridge crossing I stopped to have a closer look. Her water was clear, perhaps in the 125cfs range, with a colorful, rocky bottom. A boy was tossing lures into the hole just below the bridge, his dad watching impatiently from above. I scanned upstream and down, allowed the afternoon breeze to caress my sweat-soaked back and the river's song to connect with my heartbeat. High above, perhaps 1500 feet, there was a blue sky adorned with cumulous. Great pine, spruce and fir pocked ancient granite. I had no idea what awaited down river. I only knew that the one-lane road paralleled all way to a major artery heading east and west, the one I'd eventually take home.

After a brief chat with the boy's dad, I ventured a bit farther downriver. The water played peek-a-boo to my left, her way of acting coquettish, me trying to not stare as she sparkled. At a small pullout I again stopped. I could take no more of her games. We had to meet, properly, with me dressed for her, Seal-Dry rubber waders, my trusted fanny pack full of accouterments and a San Francisco Giants baseball cap. That is how I wanted her to feel me for the first time.

I'll spare herein many of the details of my time there, mostly because I've gone on enough about this river in my first book, *The Middle Fork-Trout Tales*. For those of you who suffered that literary calamity, this river I'd stumbled on is the infamous "'Bou". For those who by wisdom or destiny avoided my earliest attempt at producing the equivalent of Penthouse Forum letters for trout bum fly anglers, the river we now stand astride is the very first love. She who would captivate my every synapse. She who without seeming reluctance or penitence became the most demanding and rewarding force in my life. The 'Bou. She's a tributary to large drainage, one which now is held and released by almost a dozen PG&E dams on its way to the Sacramento River a little ways north of the state capitol. The entire region once welcomed great runs of steelhead and salmon. But now it's all trout. Or squawfish. Or nothing.

On that first trip, still recovering from the abject spurning I'd endured at the hands of the McCloud River and her sisters, I timidly introduced myself to the 'Bou. That evening, in the calm, shaded canyon, a tremendous hatch occurred. I'd come to learn that the fly was a Pale Morning Dun and the river enjoyed a great number of the graceful mayfly. In the pool just below where I'd set up camp, several fish were feeding casually on the ovipositing females. I didn't have the perfect fly, nor the ability to present sufficient drifts with any consistency. But I did enjoy the challenge. And finally, in the encroaching darkness, a generous trout saw in its heart to engage The Wand and I. The rise was subtle, a nonchalant tipping up, a delicate opening and closing of the mouth. It was nature reciting poetry. My setting of the hook was a panicked, flailing thrash. It was the metaphoric driveling attempt at chatting up the beautiful woman who you've admired from afar all night and for some reason *she* actually approached *you* to say "hello", and then, instead of conjuring some debonair introduction, you pathetically trip over your own tongue and somehow manage to shower the lovely lady with expectorate before she flees. What, that's never happened to you? Well then, you haven't lived.

As I was saying, my set on this fish, which turned out to be a sizable rainbow, was less than ideal. Incredibly, the hook-up lasted another ten seconds before fly and tippet parted ways. As darkness overcame my run, I reeled in and made for camp. After the obligatory self-derision I actually found some grandeur in my folly. That I had found a place where I was welcomed, where I had relative solitude and quiet, where a beautiful little river sang under the stars, where I had actually fooled a fish with a dry fly, brought a great sense of light into my heart. The feeling was as addictive as any I've known: surfing down the curling faces of waves, gliding skis over cornices into flight, powering through pitch-black ocean night under a taught spinnaker, or playing music to adoring crowds. This was the new drug, the rush needed to compel my spirit. I had found it, and it me.

That day and night would prove a turning point for me. The 'Bou would welcome me into her dramatic canyon world countless times over the next few years. Hers was the embrace I craved. Hers was the magic that awakened my soul. Hers was the bosom I ran to when I needed time to think, songs to write, tears to shed. From the complications of life, she'd shield me. From the confusion of scattering my dad's ashes into the ocean, she allowed me the time and space to grieve, and absorb my anger at having lost him far too early.

But perhaps more importantly, she taught me to live in that intangible space between real and make-believe, between sleep and wake, where triumph and failure coexist happily and creativity flourishes, where my wishes were attended to, my attentions rewarded and my love reciprocated. In time, through her caring, therapeutic embrace I almost forgot about that other woman, she of flesh and bones and black heart, who had left me for dead. This new seductress was potent beyond any I'd known or conjured. And through *her* I found a *me* I'd not known. A curious, engaged, caring and grateful lover emerged as I wandered every inch of her luscious canyon.

In time we did tire of each other. For me, I simply wanted to taste different fruit and challenge myself. For her it was as bold-faced as putting a scorpion in my tent one trip. It wasn't entirely her fault though. The men who controlled the dam upriver put in place a new flow regime that had negative effects on the overall riparian habitat in her canyon. The less water flowing through her veins, the dryer the land along her banks became. The bear and cougar I'd become almost accustomed to seeing were gone. The birds whose songs I longed for had also moved on. When it was time to say goodbye, I felt as if she knew why. But my heart ached just the same.

The air cools into evening
Still, near opaque and dancing
Invisible movement
The feast of bats
Darkness impedes
A trembling kiss
Or the whiteness of a trout's mouth

Chapter 2

An Affair To Remember

For a while there, the 'Bou and I had a fairly serious thing going. You know, it wasn't quite a relationship, but we definitely saw each other with a frequency that wasn't casual. When I needed that little shot in the arm, I went to her. She had proved the right combination of challenge and ease, which for an aspiring lover of trout on a fly rod was crucial. The art of fly fishing can be difficult enough for the relative beginner. Having a welcoming bosom is sometimes what is required to keep the stoke alive. And so for a few years, whenever I was feeling randy I went to her. Or maybe I was just needing the caring embrace of something familiar. Either way, she was close enough by, I could find my way around her in the dark and I was pretty much assured a good time whenever I visited. Was there a sense of complacency? Yea, probably. But she also knew how to smack me around from time to time. She wasn't always sweetness and light. I'd have grown bored far earlier if that had been the case.

But this story isn't about the 'Bou. It's about her smokin' hot cousin, the Middle Fork. Our introduction came as these things often do, through a friend. Stefano had visited the 'Bou and was in the town nearest her when he encountered a man in a diner. They began talking about fishing and the guy asked Stefano if he had ever been to the Middle Fork. When the answer was "no", the guy proceeded to explain how to get into a very remote area where the fishing was said to be good for a very old strain of rainbows that had been in this stretch of river for many decades. Stefano was promised solitude, a nice campsite and decent fishing. Back then, that was all that mattered. Still is, I suppose.

I'm forgetting now what Stefano's first experience down there was like, but it was enough for him to see fit introducing me to this new, willing, beautiful and mysterious *other*. Little could either of us known what that river would come to mean. For a while there, the Middle Fork is what he and I talked about even when out amongst friends in smoky San Francisco bars. Tucked away in some dark corner booth, we'd go over trips we'd just taken or plot our next disappearance into her deep, remote and foreboding canyon. This was the first place we discovered that was roadless and bereft of trails the length of her descent. Even the dirt track out there was treacherous. But once in her current she was an enthralling beauty, all narrow slots and deep, slow pools; she had amazing horizontal riffles, shelving tailouts, boulder-strewn pockets; thick hatches of summer Pale Morning Duns and caddis. The camping area was a mining claim, left mostly alone for a hundred and fifty years; a large flat along an otherwise uninhabitable canyon. The fish themselves are an oddity and there is some argument as to their genetics. Over the years, I met people who claim the rainbows are pure natives, leftover from when steelhead migrated all the way up there. The massive dam many, many miles below -the only one between the headwater and the Central California valley- was built from 1961-1968 and though the steelhead had pretty much died off in that river by then, the construction finished the job. So there is a chance that the rainbows up there are some mutant strain left over from the sea run fish. There has been a hatchery program well upriver for years but they have never been brood stock and generally are put in places where summer recreators pillage them all by the fall. There is the possibility that some of these fish made their way down river during spring floods, got stuck, procreated and made a home for themselves. But in my limited experience with these things, I've never seen a wild strain come from hatchery fish that look and behave as the Middle Fork fish do. So without further investigation, I'll claim these as natives. And no, I won't tell you where this place is for you to attempt sussing it out for yourself. Truth be told, after all the drought of the last few years, I'm guessing the Middle Fork has taken a beating, just as she has countless times. She's bounced back before and will again. As I write this story, California has experienced a wet winter with above normal snowpack, so maybe this is the beginning of another revival.

Stefano and I enjoyed a bunch of memorable adventures down there. It was a place more wild than we had known in the Sierra. The remoteness brought us in touch with a part of ourselves we'd perhaps not tapped into. At first, we swore to never venture down there solo. And for the first year or two, we stuck to that. One fall trip saw us get pummeled by a rainstorm so violent we fled fearing the river would flood the flat. On summer trips we were beaten down by the heat and exposure. Every time we went, from the moment we got down there, we were tiny, fragile things.

It wasn't until Satchel, the lab came into my life that I began to go without Stefano. As crazy as it may sound, from day one that dog made me feel safe in places I probably shouldn't have been. The Middle Fork was one of our first stops together. Her initial river outing was an off-season tailwater when she was only four months old. Her first summer was full of quick trips to mellow rivers where I trained her into the best fishing dog I've ever known. Early that fall we made our introductory trip into the Middle Fork.

And it was almost her last.

We made our way deep into the canyon on the first day, catching a few fish and allowing her time to acclimate. Maybe a mile in there is a huge pool, bending right, that requires a sketchy circumnavigation. A rock face juts up, all veiny metabasalt, on the river right side and must be climbed to the one shelf you can traverse. The shelf is plenty wide enough to walk on but midway along there is a gap that drops off almost to the river. This is where we humans use our hands to clutch the rock face while carefully stepping across the gap. I hadn't really thought about how Satchel would cross it until we were there. She had been obediently following when I stopped. After figuring that she should go first, I pressed myself against the rock and she passed me. Then I gave the command, "Satchel, GO!" She did as told, taking a couple steps and then launching for the other side of the gap. But came up just a little short. Her front paws clung briefly but when her body weight overtook her grip, she fell.

The crevice narrowed at the bottom perhaps fifteen feet below, near river level. I couldn't see her land from where I stood, but I heard it just fine. It was a sickening thud accompanied by a pained yelp. I peered down to see her crumpled on a small rock shelf in a tangle of riverside brush, trapped momentarily. It was one of the most horrifying moments I've ever endured on a river. All the potential outcomes flooded through me. The thought of having to carry her out. Or worse, what if she'd suffered a terminal injury? How would I deal with that? As I looked down at her and she up at me, my fear mixed heavily with guilt at having put us in this situation. I cannot tell you how much time passed just then. I do remember talking to her, asking if she was okay, apologizing over and over. She struggled to get her legs underneath her. She was only a few feet above the river. The only way I could get to her would be stripping and swimming in from above. She couldn't climb back up, even if she was physically able. I kept telling her how sorry I was and beseeching to please get up, get free of the tangle. As the endless seconds became minutes, the look in her eyes went from pained panic to determination. She wriggled harder until some progress was made. I still couldn't tell if she was seriously injured. She wasn't yelping anymore. But I had no idea how I'd get her out of there if she couldn't do it herself. How do you swim with a badly damaged dog in your arms?

I felt so completely out of my league, as if my idiotic bravado was finally going to turn on me. "Come on, girl," I beseeched, "You can do it. You can DO IT!" I'll never know if it was her will to live or desire to please me that compelled her, but she finally righted herself and began working through the brush to get to the river. From my vantage point I saw no blood. I had surmised that the brunt of the impact was on her hips and ass, so I watched closely how she was moving. At the river's edge, she turned and looked up at me. "Good girl, Satchel!" I called to her. She wagged her tail, scanned the river and then looked back up. "Good girl," I called again. I may have begun crying. "Get in! Go down!" These commands she knew well. She leaped into the calm pool and began swimming. I hopped over the crevice and made my way as quickly as I could to meet her. By the time I was down to the river, she was out, shaking water off. I tossed my rod and pack to the ground, squatted down, and allowed her to jump up and lick my face. Then I took a minute to rub all around her wet hips and tailbone. No whimpers or cries. Then I sat on a perfect little table rock and she leapt into my lap. The tears now flowed freely down my cheeks, my hat and glasses strewn on the rock, Satchel licking the whiskers off my face. Incredibly, I could find no discernable injury. But even as she curled into me, I could feel her adrenalin flowing. The weight of what had happened would leave scars regardless of bodily damage. Then she hopped off and sat next to me, scanning the river, looking for a fish to fool.

For years, whenever we visited the Middle Fork, upon that pool, she'd stop, look at me and wait for the command, "Go, Satchel! Get in. Go around!" at which she'd jump in the river and swim the length of the pool, always getting to bottom before me. I'd find her on that same rock, sitting full of pride and defiance, sagaciously peering upon the river's surface for a rising trout.

Some time later I was on a solo trip to the Middle Fork without Satchel. She had a medical procedure that kept her from accompanying me. I arrived late one night, set up camp and slept sound as a pound well into the morning. After some granola and coffee I got suited up and began a slow, deliberate trek into the canyon. Each pool yielded a fish or two that morning, most falling for a Prince Nymph size 16. Nothing remarkable was happening, which suited me just fine as I attempted to relax into my surroundings, the remoteness and my own fragility. I recall searching for the right balance of comfort and caution. A few hours into the day I was scaling against a rock face to get around a deep pool. I was only a few feet above the river but still leaning heavily into the rock, clutching it closely, sidestepping. Then I heard a growl. As is my wont in the wilderness, whenever an unknown or unseen oddity is felt, I yelled, "FUCK OFF!" You know, I just believe that trying to get the quick upper hand and not betray any sense of fear is the best opening salvo. My suspicion was bear or cat. I know of nothing else that growls down there. To my knowledge, there were no wolves or coyote. But something had most assuredly just growled. As my subtle introduction reverberated off rock walls, I listened for a reply. I hoped to hear something crashing into the bushes around the corner, running away. As I clung to the rock, in a pretty committed and vulnerable spot, I heard nothing for a moment. Then it growled again. Shit. In an even louder voice, one my ex-Marine, sailboat skipper dad would have approved of, I let fly, "GET THE FUCK OUTTA HERE!" Then I looked at my retreat options, conjuring just how fast I could move it the situation came to that. These options were very poor. In a place we humans are simply not meant to be, if there were a hungry, wild animal around that corner, it would have the upper hand, completely. Again I heard the growl, only this time it sounded closer and louder. Whatever it was, now it stood mere feet from me, unseen, pissed off and territorial. I slowly began backing up, trying to hold my breath; maybe if I just disappeared... Then I heard the human voice, "Hey, Buster! Get on back here! Whatchu growlin' at, dog?" I quickly scampered back to the corner of the rock and then pulled myself around it. The dog, a mangy mutt pushing eighty pounds, began a whole-hearted, throaty bark. "Shut the fuck up," I ordered as I stepped off the shelf and onto the beach below it. Just a damned dog, I thought to myself. What a pussy. The dog was running back to its master; now realizing I was no longer afraid of it. The guy was walking towards me. We met halfway down the beach. "Hey man," he began, hand outstretched. "Sorry about that, buddy."

"It's all good," I assured him as we shook hands. "Wasn't sure what it was for a minute there when I was around that corner. I'm Griff."

"Kyle. Aw shit, man," he began as we both looked back up at the rock promontory. "Yea, I didn't even know he ran off till I turned around an' he was gone." He turned downstream. "We're down there dredgin' fer gold."

"No shit. Didn't know anyone still did that down here."

"Yup," he said nodding rapidly, as if attempting to convince me his was a worthwhile endeavor. "Hell, man. Yer lucky you didn't drop into any of the holes we been diggin'." We stood in silence for a moment while I scanned my memory for any holes between camp and where we stood. I could think of none. Then he asked, "Catchin' anything?"

"Yup. Been pretty good this morning," I answered finally focusing on him. What I beheld was stunning. The guy couldn't have been more than twenty-five years old. He wore a ratty baseball cap and a week or two's worth of beard. His rubber hip boots were held together with copious duct tape. His shirt was filthy and stretched thin. None of that was particularly shocking. No, what was most freakish and disturbing was the condition of his face. His lips were horribly blistered, as were his cheeks. Through his scruffy beard I could see more bulbous scabs. The guy was in a bad way. "Been down here long?" I asked, making a real play for stupid question of year award.

A look of panic overtook him as he scanned across and then down river, then back at me. "Fuck, man. Hell yea I been down here long." He scanned his surroundings again. Then fixed his eyes on me nervously. "So where yer fish?"

"In the river."

"What the fuck?!!" he spat, his indignation was barely overridden by his confusion. "Why're they in the river, friend," he finished, trying to calm himself.

"Cuz that's where I put 'em."

"You let 'em all go?"

"Nope."

"Then where the hell are they?!"

"In the river," I answered, actually getting the impression that we could go on all day.

"So," he began, "Why'd you tell me you caught some?"

"Cuz I did."

"Okay, then you told me you let 'em go."

"No, I didn't tell you that, Kyle."

"You didn't?"

"Nope. I sure didn't. What I told you, Kyle is that I put 'em all back."

"WHY?!!" he responded, not even trying to hold back his contempt.

"Because, Kyle, the fish are not mine to keep or let go and they're sure as hell not mine to take," I answered. Part of me wanted him to understand that. The rest of me knew he never would.

"Well shit, pal. How abouts you catch one fer me? I'll eat the fucker right here!" he said, stabbing the sand with his boot. "Make a fire. Just put a stick through it and cook that thing RIGHT HERE!" It was as if he was actually visualizing the entire scenario.

"I put them all back," I said, this time more emphatically.

"Aw maaaannn," he said, pained, pathetic. "So here's the deal," he began. I took this opportunity to lift a Camel Straight from my shirt pocket. Then I offered him one, which he greedily took. I lit them both, took a loving drag from mine and then sat in the sand. "So here's the deal," he began again. "I met this guy in town a while back, maybe two weeks, and he told me he had a mining claim down here. Told me if I joined him, we'd split whatever we found, right? So I was like, 'hell yea, man!' Next thing I know we're driving all the way out here, setting up camp, draggin' all his shit way down canyon, hiking in and out every day, and we ain't found SQUAT!"

"Where you guys campin'?" I asked, scanning the river for trout.

"Up there, man!" Kyle was beginning to get animated. I just wanted to go fishing.

"Huh. Didn't see your camp when I came in last night."

"I know! It's all tucked back up in some trees. This guy said he didn't want nobody knowin' we're here."

"Well shit, Kyle. Sounds like a bad deal, buddy." I really had nothing else for him at that point. "I'm gonna head down and fish a bit more." I stood back up.

"Will you keep some for me?"

"Nope."

"Aw come on, man. I'm fucking hungry! Can't remember the last real food I ate. This guy keeps telling me we're gonna head out and go to town for food and we never do. I'm starvin', man."

"Yea, Kyle. Like I said, sounds pretty fucked up. But I'm not killing a fish for you." I felt the heartless nature in my words, but also the conviction that this was not my place to help or intervene. We began walking down the bank. Around the next corner I heard the dredge. A hundred yards farther, just beyond a short rapid, the other guy was sifting through silt river bottom. He had a homemade system on large foam pontoons, which supported a lawn mower engine. The contraption sucked the bottom onto a large square mesh tray. Several other trays lay on the bank. My first thought was how much effort it took to get it all that far down the canyon. My next was what kind of asshole tears up a river just to plunder her jewels? I was about to get me an answer to that one.

"Goddammit, Kyle!" he barked over the engine. "Where the fuck you been?" Kyle didn't respond as he stared down upon river rock. "Get back to work! Sooner we find some gold, sooner you can wipe yer ass with toilet paper 'stead o' pine needles.'"

This guy wore a large sun hat, a new pair of hippers and a long-sleeve shirt. He was in far better shape than Kyle. I nodded hello. He reached for the kill switch. "Catchin' anything?" he inquired.

"Yup."

"Well good for you. That's outstanding," he was attempting sarcasm and it wasn't of my taste. "Could we have a couple?"

"Nope." Then I turned to Kyle. "I'm heading downstream. See you in a while. Go find some gold."

As I wandered downstream I could hear the guy yelling at Kyle. Theirs was a relationship that had apparently soured.

I've omitted thus far that over the years down there I'd named all the most productive spots. Some of these monikers lacked inventiveness. "Runs 1", "2" and "3" and "The Pockets" for instance. Then we had "Freshies", "Horizontals", "Fer Sures" and "Evening Run", "Heroes" and "Low Pool". And then, down where the canyon properly steepens to the point that we would go no further, there's

"Roaches" so named because, well, it's the last, you know, spot. That's where I ended up that day, both to get away from the noise as well as the silt being stirred up. This is one of favorite pieces of river anywhere. It has, over a couple hundred feet, every kind of quality water. At the top is a steep, boulder zone perfect for simple high-sticking. Next is a series of little plunge pools. Then the river begins to turn left and two short but ideal runs have fish holding on the right bank. The wading is challenging but not sketchy. That day, as the sun began baking the canyon, knowing that I'd fish "Roaches" and then hike out to camp for a while, I worked every delicious seam, each lovely eddy, the entire right side cut bank, dead drifting the little nymph rig. I'm not sure how many fish were fooled. But it was one of those sessions where the stars line up, a certain "zone" is achieved and things actually click. Perhaps an hour and a half after walking away from Kyle, he reappeared.

"Hey, man," he said walking closer to me, a little too close for my comfort. Then, in a hushed tone. "You plannin' on camping down here?"

"Yup," I said, taking a step back.

"Fer how long?"

"Not sure. Maybe two, three nights."

"Alright," he said looking back over his shoulder and stepping in closer again. "So listen. How's about when you go to leave, I get a ride out with you?"

"How's about," I began, again taking one step back, "you get a ride out with the fucking guy who drove you in here?" I was getting agitated for a couple reasons. One, this guy's problems were not mine. And two, I hate being bothered when I'm in the zone. "I'm not giving you a ride anywhere, Kyle."

I could almost see his intent waning. He began talking again, although now it was almost a whimper. "Aw, come on, man. I'm fucking starvin' down here. Cain't tell how bad my face is, but it hurts like hell. I been trying to get him to take me to town fer a week at least. Keeps tellin' me we don't leave till we find gold."

"Well then, Kyle, I suggest you go find some gold."

"Aw man, that's just cold," he said, standing up a little straighter. I didn't disagree.

"You should get back to work, Kyle. That guy doesn't seem too stoked right now." Then I just held his eyes with mine. *I'm done*, said mine. *So am I*, said his. It was a sad, uncomfortable moment.

"Well then, could I at least have a fish or two for dinner?"

"Nope," I answered, not releasing his eyes. We stood there another few second before he turned on the loose cobble river bank and began heading back up to the low rumble of the dredger.

I fished a while longer. My hope was that they would take a break and I'd go up and fish "Heroes". But after another half hour or so, with the sun now high and hot, I gave in and began my trek back to the camp. My plan was to get a nap and then fish into the night. The walk back up was mellow, unrushed; surveying water and hoping against hope that I'd slide passed the guys without much conversation. The dog heard me first and came charging down, all exposed teeth and guttural bark. I didn't say a word as I reached down for a baseball-sized rock, and then cocked it. The dog stopped, turned and went back towards the guys. When they saw me, they again switched off the motor. This time I walked right towards the dredger, got to them and stopped. I peered into the river at a hole nearly big enough for a small car and sighed. The guy asked, "Any luck,"

"Nope," I replied.

"Bullshit," Kyle spat out. "I watched you catch a couple down there just a little while ago."

"You did, huh?" I asked, with some suspicion.

"Shit yea," Kyle said, turning towards his boss. "He's catchin' fish alright. Just doesn't want to give us none."

"Is Kyle tellin' me the truth?"

"Yup."

"Then why'd you say you weren't catchin' any?"

"Never said that," I answered flatly. There followed a moment of disruptive silence.

"To hell you didn't," he barked, and then looked over at Kyle with a smirk, as if he'd caught me in a lie.

"You asked if I was havin' any luck," I began. Then after a short pause, "And what I was doin' down there had nothin' to do with luck, friend."

"Well then," the boss began, clearly not liking our conversation. "Lemme see you catch one right there." He was pointing just upstream at the tailout of "Heroes". Without a word I began stripping a little line off the reel as I walked the seventy-five feet. The second cast was rewarded with an aggressive grab. I played and landed a beautiful, foot-long bow. As I was extracting the little Prince from its jaw, I could hear Kyle panting a few feet behind me. After admiring the fish's beauty, it slid from my hand and scampered back to the run. I stood and peered downriver at the guy and then turned to Kyle. The look on his face described agony. As I reeled in and stowed the rig, I simply said, "Kyle, you guys are doing enough damage down here to the canyon and its fish without me killing anything for you. Mining claim or not, I fucking love this place and what you guys are doing sucks." He just stood there. "I hope you get out soon. But I'm not taking you with me."

I only stopped to fish a couple times the rest of the hike out. And by the time I reached my camp at the far downstream end of the flat, I'd decided to get out of there. As much as the fishing had been really good and promised to be epic each evening, I was pretty sure I'd not relax much with those guys sharing the canyon with me. I've seen what desperation can lead a man to do. In my oldest brother's dark world of drug addiction he saw fit to steal from anybody in his path. It got him imprisoned, shot and kicked out of his own family's house. I know how bad decisions are rationalized by abject need. And I saw that need in the faces of those guys. So back at camp, I drank a beer, sat in the shade and had a good think. If they were stuck down there, stranded by something other than their own volition, I'd have helped any way I could. But the hard truth was that they put themselves down there and could get out anytime they wished. It was greed, the lust for wealth that took them there, that corrupted them to gouge holes in a wild river, that now poisoned their ability to work together as brothers. And in my thinking, that deserved no assistance from me.

It was with a heavy heart that I broke camp that afternoon. I did drive by their camp on my way out. It was a disgusting trash heap. I knew they wouldn't clean all the empty soda and beer cans, tins of beef stew, cardboard and random other shit strewn around. I'd found campsites littered like that and spent an hour cleaning before setting up my own camp. I'd cursed people just like them for debauching Nature. And as I drove the sketchy little jeep trail that led to the sketchy fire road I was glad to have left them to deal with their situation. I'll never know what became of those guys, but I'll bet it was not awesome. I never saw them again on later trips, so I'm guessing they didn't find anything. Or maybe -and this is where my near frantic imagination goes fast to work- they found a half-pound nugget, broke camp, went into town showing it to anybody they crossed paths with, hit the local saloon, got sloshed and were then led out to the woods by a local meth head with the promise of strong booze and loose women, and where they were summarily slaughtered. The nugget then became a possession of said meth head bound for Las Vegas. That is just the beginning of that story. Pick it up and run with it if you like.

Boy, it just occurred to me that based on this story one might be led to believe I had only jacked-up experiences on the Middle Fork. Couldn't be farther from the truth. If you read my first book, you'll remember the story "Wild and Scenic Indeed", which was largely about the Middle. There were many such trips. And there were a handful of wonderful solo adventures. Those were always accompanied by a stiff, unyielding trepidation; an understanding of how unforgiving the place could be. I acknowledged the heartlessness of a place that remote. And I felt my insignificance in the face of it. Perhaps that is why I kept going back. Maybe that's what I needed as an artist and angler during a time when my life morphed into that of a dad, a homeowner, a young professional. I craved the sense of vulnerability; that I could be swallowed whole in the blink of an eye. No matter why I kept going there, it was while in the hard, desolate depths of her canyon that I felt most alive, most purposeful and most exposed. It was a delirium I'd never known. Hers was a possessive lust, a consuming, wonton need for my entire attention. She would leave nothing for me to give to any other *others*. And upon returning home from a tryst with the Middle Fork, I only wanted to go back to her. I only wanted to, in some way great or tiny, have her believe that I was hers; that I was worthy. Hers was the first passion, the first all-consuming obsession. She would open my heart to the potential for even deeper, more impactful relationships. It was to her, amidst the cacophony of the other *others*, while the howling of life's responsibilities reverberated, that I swam to, spirit soaring.

She is across the water
Peering down and slightly to her right
Coy, cunning, still as a heron
Did her left cheek just push back?
If you blink she'll vanish
Into memory
Into a seam of current

Chapter 3

My Delicate Sirens

When you've explored a variety of tastes, when *others* have come and gone -some fleetingly, some for deep expansions of emotion- inevitably your attention will be drawn out, far into some special zone wherein reality and fantasy blur, where desire and capability collide and where every desperate want is confronted head-on with the sad truth that the object of your affections is simply out of your league. Wait, did I just stir up some long-buried memory of yours? Is it now thrashing on the surface of your psyche like a Metolius River rainbow? Sorry. I'd placate, but for the simple verity that I was raised by both a Marine as well as a tough Mid-West broad and therefore am not wired to coddle. But I am sorry for your heartache. Now get over it.

It was in a state bordering on ennui that I first began my pursuit of the most delicate, moody and challenging *other*. The truth is that I wasn't even looking for any one in particular. Just *something*; something to shake me out of the ennui. And while I knew there was more out there, I had no idea what might be around the next corner. Exploration and discovery had drawn me out my whole life, whether it was in a pair of hiking boots, on a bike, a surfboard, a sailboat, or later, in any one in a series of crappy trucks, traversing mountain ranges in search of moving water. Just keep going and see what's there. This same provocation lasts in me today. Then, it was more of a fire. And it led to situations great and grotesque.

When it came to fly rods and *others*, for the first decade, the fire roared. Those nearest me back then will testify that while I maintained a life with bands, jobs, friends, eventually a wife, kid and career, my attention was constantly drawn out into a world of towering pine trees, campfires, river song and discovery. What they didn't know about were my quiet times, when just surrendering consciousness to sleep, when re-entering into the next box of a calendar, sitting in traffic, in the middle of a guitar solo, it was then that the *others* came most searing, unflinching, stoic even, just there. I kept much of this to myself for years. There was just nobody to confess to.

One of my oldest friends, Stefano, was the first person I admitted my infatuation to. I knew he'd understand. He's a poet, the son of an incredible artist, raised by a woman who makes kaleidoscopic roses explode from the earth. In Stefano, there was a depth of understanding the cosmos, and a spirit consumed by a burning hunger to learn and to feel. So it was to Stefano that I confessed my lust for the *others*. And it was Stefano who at first compelled me to chase those I felt were out of my league. It was Stefano who eventually would join on these quests, sharing memories we'll hold close till the end. Some of these adventures would become part of our fabric. Some would be quickly forgotten. But they were a constant in our lives when little else was.

So one day, hoping that the whispering winds wouldn't alert my loyal mistress, The 'Bou, and that great siren The Middle Fork of my impending betrayal, I packed my little white Nissan pick-up and ventured far north, into the sunset shadow of Mt. Shasta, to Trout Country. On this trip I was pursuing a handful of *others*, prospective lust objects all, each vying for my attentions, each with undeniable attributes.

But then I saw her.

Sometimes, as bleary-eyed as we might be, regardless of how our own filters may flatter only to deceive, in spite of whatever caution we may muster, we see something that is just stunningly beautiful, attractive beyond any previously known measure. Therein lies a moment of transformation, the world as we understood it shifts on axis. That is what happened for me that morning. It should be noted that when I first espied her, it was from a sleeping bag laid unceremoniously next to the truck, atop a leaking Therm-a-rest pad, which was in turn atop a holey tarp. I'd arrived at what I thought was a legitimate campsite (it wasn't) late at night, a bit buzzed and tired (isn't that how one is meant to arrive at a new river?) and simply passed out. It only occurred to me later that as I fell asleep there was no sound. Depending on where precisely you lay your bag out, there is sometimes the rumble of passing cars or maybe wind rustling leaves. But if you're on a fishing trip and you've arrived at your river, and then you put your bag on the cold hard ground, almost always you can expect the sound of moving water. This is a sound I've grown equally addicted to and fascinated by. You'd be surprised, and most likely a little disappointed, to learn of the endless hours I've spent draped over a granite boulder or propped against a great pine tree, eyes closed, head positioned just so, listening to every texture of sound rivers make. I look at the water the entire time I'm fishing. But I only feel it when my eyes are closed. As the metaphorical cobwebs cleared that morning, from my sleeping bag I saw a perfectly silent river. I had never seen anything like it. In the calm of the morning, under pastel skies, the water simply moved. And while I was aware of no melody, no unique lyric, the water sang through texture.

I sat up and leaned against my dirty little truck.

The river was quite wide, choked in with tall grass on both sides. And while it had no obvious structure, the surface had hundreds of delicate seam lines. There was something in the bottom creating these micro currents, but nothing big enough to break the river's smooth face. No pockets. No eddies. No riffles. None of the definition I'd learned -or tried to learn- to read.

After extracting myself from the sleeping bag I set about making coffee on the tailgate of the truck. For those few minutes my attention was drawn away from the silent coquettish *other*. A part of me shied away, intimidated, unsure of a proper opening line. But once the little percolator was over heat, I again allowed myself to stare. And the more I gazed up river, then down, from one bank to the other, watching sky reflections distort on her surface, I felt drawn in a way a river had never provoked.

I was being introduced to my first spring creek. The one in question -and no I won't name her as she's in a bad way right now, improving, but needing time away from people like us- began many, many miles from where I awoke that morning. Through a multitude of guises she ends up there, winding through a wildflower meadow, a shade of green needing to be seen to be believed. But what she lacked is what struck me the most: sound.

By the time coffee was made, imbibed and allowed its dirty work, I donned waders and made my way to her banks to find some bugs were coming off. I'd come to learn later that they were Tricos, an amazing little mayfly known and adored throughout the fly-fishing world. I'd just never heard of them. Then, out in the middle, well beyond my casting range, a fish rose to eat one. The event was, unsurprisingly, silent. The swirl though, was impressive. A small fish wouldn't displace water like that. Between the rise form and myself was fifty feet of river. Behind me was maybe twenty feet of useable back cast room. There were seams of varying width and speed every ten or fifteen feet out to the fish. I shook my head and began walking upriver, thoroughly discouraged. It was the equivalent of finally summoning enough courage to actually approach an object of attraction, only to stumble, belch and pass out, a grunting, drooling barbarian before even offering a greeting. Immediately, tail wedged between legs, shoulders slumped and whatever volition I had to properly engage, wafted off in the morning zephyr.

A little ways farther upriver a fish rose closer to the bank. I went into full covert ops mode, walking low to the ground, trying to remain invisible in the tall grass. I was suddenly a cheetah. Yea, a Serengeti cheetah, defining stealth, with a doomed antelope locked in crosshairs. Every step full of purpose. Every breath composed. Through sheer cunning I approached near enough to make out the shape of the fish not twenty feet from the bank. Still crouching, I stripped line from the reel and strategized the presentation. I'd lay the size 14 Adams, deftly seven and a half feet off the fly line and delicately affixed to 3X tippet, two feet above the lurking lunker. In that moment, I foresaw my prey ignorantly tipping surfaceward and greedily slurping the smallest fly I possessed. This all transpired in my lurching, delusional imagination. The first false cast sang out over the silent river. The next, lengthening the line out, ranged over my target. The third, oh the beauty, the predatorial perfection, the final, fatal pounce, laid out into the soft morning air, alighting a few feet above the swimming log, and its fate was sealed.

Have you ever seen a fish swim sideways? I have. The first time was just then, that morning as I introduced myself to the most seductive *other*. The moment the fly landed, this trout simply swam directly to its right. It didn't turn and bolt; no, it just casually swam towards the middle of the river, sideways, unhurried, unafraid.

I think it most likely unnecessary to relate the utterance emitted. I will, though, recount that I really thought I had chance at that one. In my charming dementia I honestly believed I did everything right. So overcome with indignation was I that caution and self-awareness were thrown to the wind and I proceeded to repeat the previous scenario another dozen times over another dozen fish. I was suddenly the drunk guy in the bar wandering stool to stool, table to table blowing tequila expectorant over every unwitting beauty who dared fill my vision. Stumbling catastrophically; an unforgettable nightmare and complete embarrassment to and for everyone present, yet in the possession of the self-belief that I actually had a chance. It was an obnoxious, entirely regrettable couple of hours that haunted every sober minute of the five-hour drive home that afternoon.

In fact, it blurred my fly-fishing narrative for months to come. Years, if I'm to be totally honest.

I would revisit that river several times before fooling my first fish. Each time I'd arrive with a refreshed focus and ambition to "succeed". When the fly-fishing affliction is still fresh and new, the parameters of a "successful" trip are quite narrow and easily defined. Just go somewhere and catch something. Then, years, miles, the vastness of the universe, life's gains and losses all serve to expand the concept of fly-fishing gratification. But yes, in those early, formative years much was taken straight to the heart. The reality that rivers and their denizens couldn't give less a shit about me or my feelings was, back then, hard to accept. The trout's existence on that spring creek would be unaltered by my presence, day after day after day. Hers was the ultimate game of hard-to-get. She was teasing without even trying. And I loved it, all excited wagging of tail and obsequious fainting and fawning. Accepting her modesty took a little getting used to. I suppose I didn't want to admit my perversion. You know, what would people think if they knew? Would I become an outcast, a pariah vanquished to the fringes of fly-fishing society? And how does one get accustomed to returning from a fishing trip and admitting that no fish were caught? Or hooked? Or even properly tempted? And then, how do I come to peace with ten hours of driving, all the gas, three nights in a tent at a nine-dollar a night campground, shopping for beer and food, missing band practice, getting someone to cover shifts at work and then not even fooling one fish? That's a real quandary for a twenty-two year old.

I eventually conjured the courage to visit the local fly shop, which was in a little house just a ways east of the nearest town, run by Dave and Janice. The first time I walked in, what struck me were two things: one, the bins full of hundreds and hundreds of flies, all tied in-house and mostly size tiny. And two, it reeked of stale coffee and cigarettes. Badly. Dave and Janice were hunched over matching vises, their backs to the entrance. This, I'd come to learn, is where they could be found most days. As I retrace this place and this time right now, I feel compelled to pronounce those two the friendliest people I ever encountered in a local fly shop. Now for those of you, like myself, who've travelled around a bit and visited local shops that might not come off as the most ringing endorsement. But instead of focusing on all the droning, bitter jerks you may have confronted in fly shops, instead try to remember the fondest greeting and most pleasant conversation you ever had with a guy upon entering one, and then imagine it even cooler than that. Not to mention they tied incredibly beautiful and effective flies. It was Dave who finally explained what was required to fool fish out there. He sold me a handful of flies and sent me on my way, full of a renewed sense of hope and purpose.

That evening, when the sun ducked behind the westward ridge and the air cooled, there were an insane amount of bugs out. This was nothing new. The river back then produced "blizzard" hatches almost daily. The numbers of natural insects actually made the fishing tougher. And when the hatch or spinner fall was at its thickest, the fish had no interest in something that didn't look identical to the real thing. Take a moment and look up that word. It perfectly illustrates the challenge. The cool thing was that I finally had the fly that was as close to identical as possible. I was also using around fifteen feet of leader and tippet down to 6 or even 7X. So at least that most important piece of equipment -the one lodged between my ears- was feeling a little more in tune. As the evening turned to dusk I was working over a half dozen regularly rising fish out thirty or forty feet. On this night I had graduated from simply watching the big trout eat elegant Pale Morning Duns, to actually anticipating one tipping up to my fly. The great, overriding challenge on a big spring creek is getting a really good natural drift. As the line, leader, tippet and fly land, the river's surface immediately conspires to drag the fly. So a variety of in-cast mends must be utilized. I was slowly learning "S" mends, reach mends and pile casts. I was adjusting to tall grass on the bank behind me by dramatically raising my elbow in the back cast, and then drilling in the importance of dropping said elbow back into my ribcage on the forward movement. Little by little I felt pieces falling into place. Every few cast I'd get a drift long enough to at least have hope, fooling myself into believing I could fool a trout.

Just before dark, having moved downstream to target a fish only thirty feet out, I fell into a zone. With glasses propped on cap bill, the faintest chill in the air, not another soul to be seen, it was suddenly just the river and I. For my part there was a calming, an easier breath, less tension in my hand, wrist, forearm and shoulder. Nature's lubricant had been applied.

The fish in question was invisible to me but for a proud snout and sizable mouth displayed three or four times per minute. It was holding in four feet of water eating along a seam line that slid a foot one way and then back the other. Between the fish and I were four or five other seams, each producing micro-currents capable of deforming a decent drift. Cast after cast looked promising for a few seconds before the Light Cahill dragged just enough to produce a slight wake, rendering the drift ineffective. I'd learned to let the fly slide out of the fish's vision before up-casting, making every effort not to spook it. On maybe the twenty-fifth cast, in almost complete darkness, the fly landed in the perfect spot, the "S" mend allowed a drag-free drift, every fiber and synapse was still, and the universe held its breath. Then, from the unseen depths, beneath a night-sky reflection, the head appeared. Fortunately there was enough slack line to delay my too-abrupt setting of the hook. The fish turned and buried the little fly solidly in its jaw and displayed immediate disdain for its situation. I'd love to report on how masterfully I played this trout on light line under the dark sky. But the truth is that perhaps ten long, panicked but delirious seconds elapsed before the line was once again tension free. Slowly, and with adrenalin coursing through veins, I reeled in. I knew that the fly had been removed from the tippet. It was now too dark to bother tying on another. I had been thoroughly bested by the fish; there would be no denying that truth by substituting it with another. And yet on the walk back to my truck

I felt only victory, a sense of accomplishment new to me as an angler. A switch had been flicked and I would never be the same.

My infatuation with spring creeks would snowball over the next decade. Nick Lyons' book *Spring Creek* was published during this time. I read it over and over, consumed with a stew of admiration and envy that he had carved out such a life as to allow him an entire season plying such complex and rewarding waters and grateful that he was possessed with the writing skill to relate the experience so beautifully. Through his writing, I was with him every step, day after day, figuring out the intricacies required to fool certain fish, appreciating the swelling and retracting of particular hatches. I felt a kind of kinship, like my perversion wasn't an anomaly.

One of my first trips to the Rockies found me ensconced at Hubbard's Lodge in Paradise Valley, on the banks of Merrill Lake, perched on a hill overlooking the Yellowstone River. I was being treated to a brief, delicious taste of the good life by my extraordinarily generous and somewhat eccentric mom and step dad. I'd flown to Billings, rented an SUV and had ten days to explore. During the few days I had at Hubbard's, I fished the lake on and off for its obese and indiscriminate rainbows, and horse-packed up to Ram's Lake for the even less picky cutthroat. The morning of my last full day there one of the guides came over at breakfast and told me someone had dropped out that day for a trip to Armstrong's Spring Creek and would I like to join. I wouldn't be guided, but there was a "card" available. The Paradise Valley spring creeks are world renowned for their difficult fishing and exclusivity. This was a moment akin to me being in Hollywood and for unknown reasons having been invited to some movie star's mega-crib high above the Sunset Strip for a cocktail party, and then somebody approaching to ask if I'd like to be introduced to Kim Basinger. For those of you too young to remember her, substitute your starlet of choice; but Kim was totally, completely and irrevocably smokin' hot. And here was my chance. Nervously, I told the guide, Craig, that I would love to go along, the honor would be mine.

A couple hours later, having swung by George Anderson's shop in Livingston, I found myself along the banks of one of the most famous spring creeks of all. This is a place of legend and lore, where giant fish eat little dry flies all day, every day, where matching the hatch takes on a precision unfamiliar to most other rivers. Sure enough, on that August morning, the run I stood over had dozens of feeding trout. You could see them lying down in channels between swaying aquatic grass, finning against constant current. Then redirecting focus to the glassy surface there were little bugs, wings aflutter, haplessly drifting over the fish. In an instant, an almost effortless surge brought the trout to the fly and then left only dissipating circles of movement. When the surface regained its calm, the fish was back in its lie, awaiting the next morsel. It was so fascinating to watch I almost forgot why I was there. Kim was now right in front of me, acting as natural as any being in any situation, and I was at an utter loss as to how I should engage. She was awaiting me, having been alerted to our impending introduction, and *I* was fainting before the duel.

You've no idea how much it would please me to blather on about how I masterfully deposited little PMD patterns into unwitting trout mouths; about the astonishing number of twenty-plus inch fish that collapsed into my net. How I wish that I could truthfully relate each exquisite presentation, each casual, tipping rise, each frantic battle; I'd love to tell you that I simply strolled over to Kim and said something that provoked her to laugh so hard that the sun-dried tomato dip she was eating came out of her nose, and that once having regained her composure she asked if I'd like a tour of the mansion, which inevitably ended up with our clothes -yes, my Perry Ellis navy blue linen suit and her Gucci floral, spaghetti-strap sundress- draped haphazardly around the hot tub, the two of us lost in each other's eyes, sipping the finest champagne, professing every desire our souls possess, our skin melting together, claiming there and in that moment an undying devotion; she'd leave Alec Baldwin for me, and I, oh the sacrifices I'd make; I'd quit my job doing sub-rosa surveillance for an insurance investigator in San Francisco; abandon my first floor, air vent studio apartment; jettison my Bukowskian existence and every artistic endeavor; her dreams were now mine, and my previously held ambitions were dust in the Santa Ana winds; I'd accompany her, slavishly, selflessly from one exotic movie locale to the next. My guitars and amps would be sold at far less than their market value. My rattling pick-up truck with its glove box full of parking tickets would be left in a bus zone. I'd hug family and friends 'goodbye', swearing I'd write and to not worry for me, professing that I was making the right decision; I'd leave behind my fly rods to, wait, what? Okay, now hold on one cotton pickin' minute here. That's just crazy talk. I mean, she's hot and everything, but I'm standing on the banks of Armstrong's Spring Creek. And the fish are eating. Get a grip, man.

As a compassionate soul, I'll spare you all the details of the next five hours. I will tell you that I went through approximately three dozen flies, no fewer than twelve hundred and fifty presentations and in the neighborhood of ten smokes with a total of zero takes. Oh, I had fish look at my flies. But it was more of a sneer, an arrogant, contemptuous glance than an edible interest. This didn't happen a couple times; it was at almost every new fly. It was a cursory inspection on their behalf, almost as if they wanted to keep me utterly engaged only to deny my carefully placed offering time and time again, to audaciously refuse every token of my adoration. Kim had spoken, without uttering a word.

Sometime in the late afternoon an elderly woman came strolling down the trail. I was sitting on the bank, pouring over my fly box, insistent on finding some answer to a question not even fully formed in my head, most likely muttering nonsensically to mayflies blowing passed, cigarette smoke wafting from under the bill of my cap, a full inch of ash poised to fall into said fly box, neck bright red from being in this position most of the day. She was chipper. I was not.

"Hey there, fella!" she chimed, having stopped mere feet from the statue that had become me. I'm supposing I grunted and mumbled some unrecognizable response. She said, "You been doing any good?"

"Nope."

"Oh that's too bad. Whatcha usin'?"

"Everything," I said as I looked up at her.

"Aw geez." There was true compassion in her tone. As she paused she scanned the surrounding river and its valley. "These fish can be tricky to fool sometimes."

The friendliness in her voice and seeming understanding of my reduced state snapped me out of my personal hell. I stood up. That's when I fully took this person in. She was seventy if a day. No more than four-and-a-half feet tall, possessing the facial features of a gnome. I love gnomes. She made me feel tall, something I've never been accused of. I flipped my glasses up, looked her square in the eye and asked, "Have you caught any today?"

"Weelllll," she began. I knew she was trying to be polite but was about to drop a bombshell. "Yes, I have."

"How many?"

"Oh, a bunch."

"Cool. You must be really good at this," I said, no doubt sounding like a petulant child.

"You know, this place isn't easy. These fish see it all, everyday. They get pretty keyed in too." She stopped and looked beyond me, at the water I'd been fishing. "Yea, you got some risers out there, don'tcha?"

"Been like this all day."

She reached into her vest and pulled out a box. When she opened it I could swear I heard angels sing. Inside were rows of tiny flies, ten or twelve of each, hundreds if you added them up. She plucked two from one row and delicately placed them in my palm. "These are emergers. I can see from your patch," she said pointing at the overflowing lamb's wool on my vest, "that you've been using duns and spinners." Holy crap, grandma was speaking my language! "What you need to know about these fish is that even though they'll eat off the surface, they'd way rather sip something just under. AND, strange as it sounds, if something is an inch under the surface it's harder for them to get a good look at it." I'm sure my substantial eyebrows raised. "You see," she continued, in full shaman mode now. "If something is just under the surface it has a reflection behind it that blurs definition from the fish's perspective. They see the bug but also a distorted shadow of it, so they can't see the fly as clearly. When it's *on* the surface all the fish sees is the outline, even though it's perfectly defined. But even an inch under, it's like the fly is in a mirrored box. It's so important to imagine how everything looks to the fish, you know. Not just how *we* see it or how we *want* it to appear. From the fish's perspective, the more it can see but the less it can see *clearly*, that's the idea. We want to present something in a way that so to the fish, it looks..."

"Okay! I got it," I finally interrupted. We might still be there today if I hadn't. "I just never thought of it in those terms," I finished, trying to assume a more calm tone.

"Alright, it's just that you were staring at me like I was speaking gibberish. Wanted to make sure you understood. That's all. So put a tiny bit of floatant on one of these and start fishin'. It'll sink after a few casts."

"How about you show me how it's done?" I asked, hoping as the words fell that I didn't sound challenging.

"Oh, dear," she began softly. "I'm on my way home. Flying out in a few hours. The river's all yours."

"Uh, okay. I'll give it a go."

"You'll do great. Just remember what I've explained. It'll work."

With that she kept walking, this diminutive, generous sage-gnome.

There were indeed a few fish still rising in the lowering, early-evening light. I slid back into the river and began casting. Below me was some kind of old weir that probably supported a wheel back in the day. Now it just held back a little piece of the creek, creating a nice deep run above. I was waist deep with even deeper water just in front. The trout were spread out, each coveting a slot in the river grass, each rising with regularity. The cast to reach them wasn't long or especially technical. I was river left, casting over my right shoulder and putting a little reach mend into each presentation. The tricky bit, the thing one must remind oneself of on every pass is to wait until the fly and tippet has long since cleared the fish's view before picking up to cast again. With the new fly affixed and my vigor renewed it only took a couple dozen attempts before a worthy offering was made. In the late afternoon light I only saw the fish move to the fly at the last second. And I'll never forget what it looked like to finally watch a big spring creek trout approach, convinced and without reserve. This fish would eat my fly, like it or not. My immediate and urgent task was simply to not remove the fly before it was eaten. As time stood still, my heart skipped beats, the fly vanished into the vast white mouth. The ensuing battle was long and tense. Much of the time I was convinced the fish would outlast me and my knots. This trout was significantly over 20". The fly in its mouth was smaller than any I'd ever employed. With each jump, each heaving, exaggerated headshake, I was sure the tiny hook would come dislodged, or that the tippet would come undone. But eventually I felt the great fish tire, my net was made to ready and in one lifting move the fish slid in. My net at the time was a classic teardrop deep basket style. The fish folded deeply in. I did take a picture that turned out pretty cool. Then the fish was released.

I looked upstream and down to see if I had witnesses. I did not. The emotion of the moment coursed through me and then out into the warm breeze easing its way down canyon. I exhaled deeply, allowing my breath to come one with the wind. I'd learn later of something called the "twenty-twenty club" and that I had joined it. This is for those who have landed a twenty-inch fish on a size twenty fly. It would be many years before I fully realized what a rare feat it is. But on that day, waist deep in Armstrong's Spring Creek I would do it not once, but twice. There was a third chance, but I'd blow it. The second one that was landed and the one that got away were both witnessed by another guide and his client just downstream of me. After that one shook me off, he casually asked what I was using. And I told him with total honesty that I didn't know. I'm sure he thought I was the biggest asshole ever encountered on a spring creek, which were that assumption true would make me a remarkably tremendous asshole. But I really didn't know what the fly was. I still don't. I'd describe it to you but I'm an asshole.

The next morning, while having breakfast and plotting what I'd do after checking out, Craig again approached telling me he'd had a cancellation for the day. He said he'd already shopped for lunch, had a card paid for at Nelson's Spring Creek, a neighbor of Armstrong's and if I wanted to go I'd only have to give him a tip. This was the no-brainer of the year. After packing the rental Ford Explorer with all my stuff I followed him out to the creek. Nelson's was even smaller than Armstrong's, more braided, with defined holding water everywhere. Craig, after hearing all about my flailing the previous day, took it upon himself to teach me, properly, how to fish spring creeks. It was a day of handpicking rising fish under a cumulous-pocked blue Montana sky. There were other people out there that day, but they came and went and we fished wherever we pleased for whichever trout compelled us. This day would prove to be pivotal in my ascension as an angler. I'd never been taught about downstream presentations, never had the theory instilled in me that if at all possible make the first thing the fish sees be your fly, not the tippet or line. There are several ways to accomplish this, none of which I'll bore you with here, not to mention that in Britain I'd be hanged and quartered for utilizing these techniques.

The first hour or so with Craig was tricky. You see, I thought I kind of knew what I was doing. And yea, while my casting mechanics were okay, my theory of presenting to spring creek trout was rudimentary at best. So our morning consisted of him breaking down concepts I thought were fairly sound. He was patient but demanding. He knew where I was as an angler, could tell I was aspirational, and after a little while became comfortable with working me pretty hard. These are all guiding techniques I use today. It should be noted that this session with Craig was the first time I'd ever been guided. I loved watching how effortlessly he tied knots, how he was constantly searching the water and air for clues. He was as comfortable in his element as I was intimidated by it. Each feeding fish was an equation to solve. We'd spot the snout of a large brown tucked in next to some clump of exposed river grass and then set about strategizing which cast and mend would get it to eat. Most of the day we went between a little speckled-wing caddis and the cripple version of the Pale Morning Dun mayfly. We were using around thirteen feet of leader and tippet. I was fishing my first proper fly rod, the Orvis HLS eight-foot six-inch four-weight, Poetry, which turned out to be the perfect stick for the spring creeks; just enough backbone to cast accurately and plenty of softness to protect fine tippet against large trout.

I'm not sure how many fish we caught that day. At some point after lunch I smoked a little grass after which many details tend to blur. The journal entry from that day was written from the reclined passenger seat of the rental, where I'd attempt to sleep that night, just outside the west gate of Yellowstone National Park. By that point I had long since lost the volition to include many specifics. But I am quite sure the day I spent with Craig was as impactful as any during that first decade I was fly fishing. And as I write this I feel a little sadness that he and I didn't stay in touch; I'd love for him to know what his instruction meant -and still means- to me. We should all encounter mentors such as Craig. This fly-fishing thing is plenty complicated. It pains me to think about what a crappy tip I must have given him; but no matter the sum, I'm sure it constituted half of my spending money for the next week.

My deep love affair with spring creeks is still very much with me. Over the last few decades I've fished them whenever possible. There are two very near where I live now, both fickle, both challenging and entrancing. But this *other* has been lusted for, pursued, romanced and seduced throughout the Rockies, the Sierras, in Vermont, as far south as Patagonia and now practically in my backyard. And just as that first one sang to my heart, so too have the rest. The melody resonates, swirling in the most tender regions of my soul, singing seductive sirens songs, knowing whatever music I'd heard before or since, theirs is the most captivatingly beautiful.

Chapter 4

The Meaningless Tryst

We all know that not every encounter, regardless of its perceived intimacy, its immediate import, will stand the test of time, distraction, personal erosion. Some will come and go like afternoon zephyrs roaming the Deschutes canyon. In the moment they'll have significance. Perhaps they radiate beauty uncommon to your realm. Perhaps they're the only one that will have you, when others have sent you away. Or maybe you simply feel like playing in the dirt once in awhile. While the softness, grace and beauty of *others* you're most familiar with possesses you, every now and again you crave a meaningless tryst. It's what creates balance and counterbalance in your world. For how can anything hold great and true meaning without understanding the things that hold practically none? Oh, they matter. I'm not claiming they don't. But in the context of the universe that is your energy, your belief in fate and Karma, the surety that resides in your heart, these *others* can come and go with almost zero effect.

This concept took some time to form in me. I was working my way through river systems, staying with some year after year, some for only a visit or two. Why I went back to one over another had something to do with the quality of fishing, but there were other factors as well. I often times craved solitude, a break from all the other elements of my life, including people. Sometimes I went looking for a physical challenge; I wanted to come back bruised and torn, sore in places I didn't know could hurt. Other times it was one fish. I wanted to search out, romance, seduce and capture just that one, the one lurking under a log at the tailout of a McCloud River pool, or a spring creek trout that always held the same station during certain hatches, a lie that my mediocre casting skills made seem unreachable. And still other times I packed the truck with camping and fishing gear with little intent on fishing. I wanted to be alone with my guitar and writing pad. I wished only to be left to sing and write and cry. When the cruelness of the world lorded over my psyche, I went to a river. I went to ask the great questions, to vent frustrations. It was my version of lying supine on a sofa in a shrink's office. Only I never once felt the river judge me. It never pressed me to return next week. Never told me there were pills to alleviate my discomfort. And it never sent me a bill.

For a certain period, there was this one *other*. She was not far away. She was seasonal at best. And she served the purpose. Ours was a tryst, or as the kids say nowadays, a 'booty call'. I always knew that nothing more or less would come from our time together. She wasn't intriguing, but nor was she ordinary. Let's call her 'Off-Season Beautiful'. It's kind of like how an otherwise bland woman can put on some cut-offs and any top that might feature whatever chest she has, and she goes to a race track during an event weekend. She strolls the pits and paddock, amongst all the seething testosterone, revving engines and exhaust fumes and suddenly she's a beauty queen with lascivious, drooling stares following her every step. I suppose the same can be said of women on rivers. Can't tell you how many times I've had a couple gals in my boat, and as we row passed some guy who has hiked in and now stands in a riffle attempting to fool a trout he notices them and practically drops one rod to grab another. His ogling can be felt from the near side of the river to the far. I'll lean forward so as to almost breathe down their necks and say, "Damn, ladies, you must be lookin' goooooood today." So anyway, I think you get the point here. Or do you? I have convoluted it, haven't I? What I'm trying to say is that the *other* in question had attributes, one of which was that she was available to me when other *others* weren't, and *that* was her beauty secret. Her name is the Lower Stanislaus River. I'm naming her because I couldn't really give less a damn about who goes there now. We're done. I'm utterly and completely devoid of any emotions towards her. How can anybody care about a river with some thirty dams obstructing her natural flow, whose every movement is controlled, whose beauty is trampled upon for man's need to air-condition and fill swimming pools?

Back in my formative years as an aspiring angler, such things didn't affect my perspective. She was there, the Lower Stan. She'd have me when other *others* were off limits. Her charms put a rose-tinted lens into my polarized fishing glasses. And so I went to her. Four or five times a year I'd make the short drive from San Francisco, or later, our house in the 'burbs, leaving around five in the morning. I'd be knee-deep in her frigid, mud-colored currents within a couple hours. And there were some nice fish to fool. On the stretch I frequented, she had a special regulation under which only single barbless hooks were allowed, and she was closed to all fishing from mid-October until New Year's Day to allow what few steelhead and salmon still returned to spawn in the pathetic, ruptured river she'd become. Another dam story if there ever was one. In the forty or fifty days I spent on her polluted shores, I only ever saw a few steelhead, including one that ate a small egg pattern and positively tortured the fine bamboo rod and rickety CFO reel I was using before ultimately breaking off clear across the river. It was an ass kicking of biblical proportions. Most of my time with her was spent drifting Sparkle Pupae in riffles and runs, picking up from three to ten fish a day. The trout were all wild, beautiful creatures. Most were in the foot range with a few pushing sixteen inches. I can hardly recall a less spectacular fish. They were just there. I was there. We got it on a little, but I left nothing of myself with that canyon.

And yet I think I loved her, in the very shallowest way. Or maybe there's more to this story. I should really have thought this one out. But let's see where it takes us...

I suppose it embarrasses me some to admit this now. I began this book with idea of featuring the rivers of deep impact, the ones I longed for and craved, the ones that stirred my soul. So how the Lower Stan found its way into my writing psyche mystifies. And yet here we are, me feeling soiled, guilty on some entirely base level. But she deserves more. She, at the very least, should be acknowledged as the beauty she once was. I should remind myself that what's become her is in no way her fault. Before we showed up with our deplorable greed, or compulsive desire to water decorative lawns and stay cool on hot days, she ran clear and free, home to great runs of anadromous fish, her banks populated by warring tribes of Native Americans. Her origins were nearly a hundred miles and eight thousand feet above. There, where granite promontories dominated as far as the eye can see, channels were gouged and her waters began a dramatic descent towards the Central Valley. If I were to overlook all the ugly, massive concrete structures placed to bind her, there is still a stunning beauty there. I've known her stretches upriver of the dams and she is pure joy up there. Those areas are where I spent quite a lot of time in the early days. There were wonderful campsites along the river, plenty of places where Fish and Game planted stupid fish for me, the stupid fisherman. But there were also long stretches tucked back away from the road where some wild fish resided. I found rainbow, brown and brook trout, not in tremendous size or numbers, but plentiful enough to entertain.

But we digress.

It's the *Lower* Stan which we refer to in this story, the one of the "off-season" beauty secret, the one only made pretty for lack of viable options, made lust worthy by comparison to her surroundings. All my other *others*, the ones that compelled my every angler sense, were closed during the time of the year when the Lower Stan beckoned. And so it was to her I ventured in the grey, short days of winter, to a canyon full of leafless trees, shrouded in winter's ground fog. Occasionally I visited on sparkling February days, when the sun's vague warmth found its way through layers of clothing, through my own skin and into a weary heart. My favorite zone down there required a decent little hike in. On the coldest days of winter, with the grey wall hanging low to the oak trees and drooping grass, there was a special silence to her canyon. I'd stop walking for a few moments and just listen. The river's soft hum was still down there; I just couldn't hear it through the muffling fog. Then from one step to the next the song would press through. She was down there, waiting. And like any good mistress, she cradled me in times of need, offered the soft bosom of care.

Twenty years ago a terrible tragedy struck the small coastal town where I was raised. Four young men, all from the area, died when the truck they were in flew off a particularly dangerous stretch of road. We had all driven what we refer to as the 'Mountain Road' hundreds of times. The winding, tree-lined "Panoramic Highway" between Stinson Beach and Mill Valley. Over the years many cars have slid -or flown- off and many lives changed in that instant. Or ended. I had one such experience. Two weeks before I turned eighteen, in the fall of 1982, I was up on that road with two friends. They were in the back seat, a boy and a girl, doing what you'd expect. I was driving drunk and high. The car was a 1982 BMW 528e, the first year of its production and it still maintained a waft of 'new car smell'. My mom had left me with the keys. I was an idiot. Wonder what that made her. The three of us, Joanie, Stefano and myself, left the road, Led Zeppelin blaring from Blaupunkt speakers, at a great rate of speed. There was an old redwood tree, probably eight feet in diameter, peacefully emerging from the moist earth twenty feet below the road on a steep hillside. The car clipped a small tree and turned upside down as it slowly rotated. Then it wrapped around the redwood, the driver's door taking the impact. None of us wore seat belts, just like the four young men thirteen years later and less than a mile up the road. The collision was so severe the great and proud tree buckled under the force, snapping where the car hit it. As the tree folded under the weight of German sheet metal and steel engine, the car fell to earth below it right side up. I ended up in the passenger seat, a badly damaged version of the self I'd been seconds before. Miraculously Stefano and Joanie were all but unscathed, the rear seat are having been spared the brunt of the trauma. My seat, the driver's, was protruding through the open sunroof. The entire driver's compartment was gone. The car had quite simply folded itself around the tree. More bones than not on my left side above the belt were broken or dislocated. I would spend the next six months healing. But I'd never completely recover, physically or mentally. As I've grown older some of the injuries to my shoulder ache for no good reason. I'll rub the joint or massage the knot in my collarbone, a calcium deposit where body tried to mend itself. My entire left shoulder assemblage hangs an inch lower than the right. The ribs are still tender to the touch some days. And on those days, I'll reflect on the crash, sometimes for five seconds, sometimes for an hour, head buried in hands, overwhelming shame squeezing me.

Why do I bring this up now? Well, because I am still alive, unlike Ian, Eli, Matt and James. And they were good kids. One bad judgment cost them and those who loved them dearly. I, on the other hand, was a shit head, a spoiled, unsupervised punk. I wish I could say that after the crash I did a bunch of soul searching and that I found God or God found me, or that a revelation occurred. But no, I pranced around like some great hero returned from a bloody battle.

And the really screwed up thing is that the deranged town I lived in at the time, Mill Valley, actually treated me as such. So instead of learning a lesson, I felt empowered by the attention. Yea, it was bad situation, made worse by my upbringing. I don't even know where my mom was the night of the crash. And my dad, the man who really should have done more to at least attempt teaching me something about life and how it should be lived, showed up at the hospital and the first question he asked the attending doctor was if I'd be able to play golf again. It's a moment frozen in my memory, etched indelibly. Even through the Demerol haze I remember the doctor turning to my dad and saying, "You should really be concerned with other things right now, Mr. Marshall." The he redirected his focus to me and finished, "And by the way, no, he won't." I'd never heard anyone talk to my dad with that tone of voice. It was full of stern judgment. The doctor was not in the least intimidated by my dad, the ex-marine, nor was he impressed with the local news celebrity, the tan, handsome, muscular Bob Marshall. He thought my dad was an asshole and there was no hiding it. That night should have been a turning point in my life. I should have woken up the next day simply happy to be alive, professing a new outlook, a blossoming appreciation for everything I'd been spared. That the passengers of the car that I idiotically speared into the forest walked away is something that will never resonate. We all should have died. But if there was a God, he'd have seen to it that I lived, that I had to carry the burden of my stupidity, my lack of respect for others, and spend my remaining days suffering for it, trying to help others escape their own moral ineptitude by spreading the word of my salvation, the Phoenix that had become me, lending the only thing I still possessed -a perspective on the actual important aspects of life- to others so that they might not make the same mistakes I made. If I hadn't been so full of myself, perhaps others in my community, my sphere, would have seen how screwed up I was at the time of the crash and recognized that even though we grew up in an area of affluence, we were no different, no more immune to self-provoked tragedy and its ensuing aftermath than anyone else. But alas I wasn't that person. Either by genetic coding or worthless parenting I didn't learn an important lesson, and therefore I had nothing to pass along that might keep others from making similar mistakes. And so one night, thirteen years later, when the guys flew off the road, I understood the terror in their last seconds -maybe minutes- before the last breath. I knew what it sounded like. I've heard the horrified screams. And the sound of shattered trees, glass and lives.

The morning after their accident I went to Stinson to be with my mom and sister. We had breakfast and talked about the heaviness, the heartache, the confusion, the time it would take before there would be healing. While the guys who had died were younger than my sister and I, we knew them. They loved to surf. They were well liked and thought of as caring, friendly members of the community. And so I asked the question, "Why, God, why these four? Is this your way of settling a score?" And then, as if I actually believed there is a God, the rant went on, "If so, you're not just an asshole, but a coward to boot. I'm still here! Why didn't you take me when you had the chance? I've served no one and nothing since. And now this?!! You suck, man."

It was with those thoughts, still taking shape, still forming what would become my own new lease, that I fled to the river.

It was February, only a week or so after my sister's birthday. I had a son of my own, eighteen months old. And I was lost, wracked with stomach-tightening sadness. My soul was being tortured. And I went fishing. It was all I knew to do. Not to get my mind off it, but to force myself through the pain and hurt, to not allow the distractions of life to ease my suffering. And it was to the Lower Stan that I went. It was one of those days down there, with the ground fog lying still and heavy, its penetrating cold finding my bones. And her quiet, grey beauty embraced me, allowed me to cry and scream into the frigid air. The canyon was mine that day. No other cars were by the gate so I knew I was alone. And I let loose with my tirade. Through my own chagrin at not having learned proper lessons by my own stupidity, through the haunting concept that if I'd been a better person, a more responsible young man, that maybe, just maybe future generations could have made better decisions. The canyon absorbed my anger and my shame. The sobbing and words dissipated into the grey mist.

And then she spoke.

Our conversation that day is and will remain a private one. But I will relate that it was as profound an experience as I've ever had with Nature. And I will also relate that it reinforced my conviction that there is no God. For some of you, I know that this will be as far as you get in this book. By no means do I wish for that to be the case, but understand the potential affront in those words. If that's the case, then thank you for making it this far, and I wish you well. I will not elaborate any further on this conviction other to say that in the place of an organized-religion style god to believe in, Nature filled that void. In the canyon that morning I found my church. And while those of you who have spent your lives in actual churches or mosques or caves etched into cliff faces might find this statement spurious, I stand by my revelation and I will continue to worship only Her. I fault no one whatever it is that gets him or her through the day. Please give me the same understanding. For in the canyon walls that morning there was the healing, forgiving hand as I imagine conventional religious types may have felt. Only it wasn't God. It was Nature. And please spare me the argument that Nature is God, that God is Nature. Just think about the ridiculousness of that one for a second.

So here we are. I've just spent the last few hours writing something that went utterly off the rails. And you've spent precious minutes reading it. Aren't we the fools? I suppose now it's fair to say that the affair I shared with the Lower Stan was not meaningless in the grandest scheme of things. In as much as I moved on, a little piece of her canyon lives on with me. While several other revelations occurred both before and after my days with her, it was that one particular morning when a true spirituality emerged in me. It was the first time that Nature spoke back. And it may have been the birth of a man that I actually like. It may have been 'day one' of the rest of my life. And maybe it's because of our time together that I became a good father to my boy, a better friend, husband, son, and brother. So yea, I guess this *other* deserves a better moniker, one better fitting her ultimate effect. I just can't think of one right now.

I do some mornings, when it's cold and damp out, think about just throwing my fishing stuff in the truck, grabbing the dog and heading out to the Lower Stan. Then I remember I live in Oregon now. That would be an awfully long drive. So instead, I go to river nearby, one that sits in a canyon under a dam with silty, brown water and rainbow trout, not entirely dissimilar to the Lower Stan. I find a rock to sit on, scratch the dog's head between her ears, my version of a pew. Then I close my eyes, and there she is, Nature.

Blankets of grey surrender
Towers of green welcome
Ribbons of blue entrance
Arching bodies of gold pirouette
A blackened heart awakes

Chapter 5

The Greatest Love

After years of being drawn out of normalcy by the siren song of the *others*, after satisfying curiosities, cadding about like a man possessed by a lack of self worth, being alternately adored and rejected countless times, I began to feel the need to settle down. Even though my heart was open and full of light, somewhere in my psyche I knew that the vagabond life I'd been living, the one which found me traipsing from the Madison to the San Juan, to Pyramid and Eagle lakes, up and down the spine of the Sierra Mountain Range would have to slow. I was becoming a father, had given up the rock star dream and its associated random "day jobs" to instead focus on making a career for myself and a "stable" life for my first wife, Theresa and our impending family. We were still living in San Francisco, surrounded by an amazing crew of friends and family. I was playing tons of music, mostly on my own or with buddies, but the last of my bands had been broken up. This proved a much harder transition that I'd expected. To go from the world of rehearsal, travel, sound-check, gig, break-down, back in the van, next show, repeat, to a life of just kind of hanging out made be feel a little batty. My time of weaning off the life of a gigging musician created a hollow in my spirit I wasn't quite prepared for. I had rationalized the life I was attempting to forge, but certainly not been prepared for what it would feel like. It felt crappy. As months wore on and my daily routine began to mesh with what I felt was my plan, the need for artistic satisfaction, my craving for a muse got stronger and more difficult to keep at bay. Were I a young man of better means or for that matter had any concept of the world of Zen Buddhism, I'd have been a poster boy for a monk convincing me that I needed to breathe out the world I'd known and breathe in the world I was embarking on; smile at what I loathed; embrace the difficulties; accept your path as the one you were intended to trod...

As it was, I found little bits of solace on rivers. Back then it was still mostly the 'Bou and/or the Middle Fork for three or four days at a time. And it was on those trips that I began to accept; accept that my dad wasn't there to celebrate my wedding day at the little Cruising Club where he'd once been commodore, that he would never meet my first kid; that my dream I'd coddled half my life of traveling the world, guitar in hand would not happen; that a more traditional life was unfurling before me. Something about those rivers, their canyons and meadows spoke back to me when I asked what I felt were life's great questions. Theirs was the comforting bosom I easily rested upon, listening intently to the heartbeat, the long, easy breaths. It was there I realized that what I missed from my life as a performing musician was not the attention or adulation, but the sense of celebration, ceremony and catharsis that was shared between the crowd and me. It was never the applause I craved, it was the moment when I felt connection through movement, sweat, smiles and rhythm, much like really good sex. The funny thing is, when I was actually going through all the rigors of being in a struggling, aspiring band, I thought it was about playing bigger venues for more people, making more money and basking in the adoration of strangers. I was an idiot. Rivers taught me that. On rivers I found the same emotions, the same struggles and victories; the same celebratory moment, only a bit quieter. The 'Bou and Middle Fork in particular assisted through much of this time in my life. It helped that I had a relatively flexible work schedule and could disappear for little stretches of time. Thankfully, Theresa appreciated what I was going through; that the transition wasn't going as smoothly as we may have hoped. And so rivers became my shrink, church, nightclub, best friend and partner in crime, my blissful distraction. They beckoned, always seeming to know when I needed them the most; what we each needed to offer in return.

Then one day, that changed. As inexplicably as when the first snow falls, when a rogue wave charges up a beach, when a heart stops loving... it just kind of ended. At first my apathy towards the 'Bou and her horny cousin, the Middle Fork caused a sadness and confusion. I knew I was enduring some kind of a loss through the disconnect. And in that sadness I was too shortsighted to recognize that I was being given the volition to reach out, to find new challenges and rewards beyond their canyon walls. There was still a heaviness of heart when I first turned my back on them to search out other *others*. And when I lay in my tent on the banks of any new river, there was still their song co-mingling; the chords they had strummed resonated no matter where I was.

My first foray into the area known as Trout Country was chronicled in an earlier chapter. And so I won't belabor it herein. But it was on that trip that I first laid eyes on the McCloud River below the dam. I'd gone to what is referred to as Ash Camp, a small flat where Hawkins Creek enters the main stem a couple miles below the reservoir. It is a well-known area. The Pacific Crest Trail comes in there from the southeast and crosses a cool footbridge on its way westward. The camp consists of four sites. There is a pooper but no running water. On that first trip, I arrived at dark, set up my tent and passed out. In the morning I allowed the river's melody to find its place in me before getting out of the tent. And even as I could still hear the 'Bou's whisper, this river had a poetry in its song; the more I listened, the more layers of complexity and meaning came through. Something in it touched a part of me until then left alone by the *others*. It would be a while before I properly allowed this one in. And she me.

That first day of fishing was a complete and utter bust. I splashed upriver and down, slapping the poor, turquoise water with all the same junk I used to great effect on the 'Bou. I stumbled over boulders many times the size of what I'd grown used to. No fish were fooled or seen. The McCloud, in all her majestic bitchiness threw me a blank and sent me on my way, as uncaring and unaffected as you can imagine. I had never felt so chucked to the curb.

I would have to go back through my journals to report on exactly how long it was until my next visit. As related in a previous chapter, on the same initial trip to that part of the state I encountered a spring creek that compelled my fly-fishing aspiration for a while thereafter. And I still visited the 'Bou as well as her cousin, the Middle Fork. But I do believe that in the fall, a little over a year after my first sighting of the McCloud, I slunk back into her canyon one miserably wet and cold night. I had gotten Satchel, the yellow lab. I remember because it was with her that I crawled into the back of my truck in the smallest hours of the morning as the rain drummed the canopy. And it was with her that I wandered the wet, mist-draped canyon floor the next day. We had driven an extra forty-five minutes on the old dirt road to get deep into the throat of her canyon, down to the campground known as Ah-Di-Nah. I was now venturing into some next-level zone of fly-fishing legend and lore. While my time on the Silver Fork, the 'Bou and the Middle Fork had been off the well-worn angler's path a little bit, now I was to rub shoulders with history, tradition, the very soul, art and poetry of angling with a fly rod. And I was entirely unprepared.

This time she didn't spit me out with the same level of contempt. I had, it should be noted made a considerably sterner effort this time; I brought a handful of flies I'd never tried, drove deeper in, and fished a long, sodden, sleep-deprived day. I had given her a signal that my commitment was, while getting hammered, very much more significant than on my previous visit. And even as I struggled, both physically and spiritually, warmth was emanating from me to her, and she to me. That day, sitting on a shiny boulder the size of a small house, staring up the towering and densely pine-covered ridges, mist hanging playfully, tauntingly in the trees, a passion I was unaware I possessed sprung from my spirit. Most people that become anglers have experienced this instance. Maybe it was the first trout you watched eat a fly off the surface of a lake, or when you made contact with your first steelhead. For me it was on that rock when I first felt a river really breathe me in. That was my moment as an angler when it made sense that I was supposed to be right there, right then; that regardless the sacrifices and tumult my life as an angler would no doubt require and inflict, every bit would be worth it and, as strange as it may sound, it would be understood and accepted by those nearest me. I knew that if I could only describe how that moment felt they would get it. What I'd later learn is that the more I tried to explain the meaning of what I felt, the less it would make sense; and the more I just silently lived with it, the more I would communicate what that sensation meant.

Yea, I had fallen in love. Just when a merciful universe may have let me attend to my wife, our infant son, my career; instead I was exposed to something compelling beyond imagination, and this force would doom almost everything in its orbit. For the next fifteen years.

I suppose it's only fair, for those of you unfamiliar with the McCloud River, to give her a bit of an introduction. But first, there is an amazing book you should read called "The Entirely Synthetic Fish" by Anders Halverson. It was published in 2010, closer to the end of our affair than the beginning. The book is about the rainbow trout hatchery and stocking programs that have, well, you know what, I'll just leave it at that. If you're interested in such things, you should totally read it. The book begins with an explanation as to why such programs were ever even deemed necessary and what happened on the early explorations west to try and find a suitable fish with which to attempt replenishing the rivers of the east that -lo and behold-

modern man had completely screwed. It was on the McCloud that they found their strain. There is, of course, so much more to the story. But the end result is that the McCloud River rainbow has become the most traveled trout ever. If you catch a rainbow in Chile, its origins are in the McCloud Canyon. Same for New Zealand. And on and on. The fish in the river do not grow massive. There are not gazillions of them. Even in a river with good spawning tributaries, solid hatches and decent flows, they are just not one of those fish that proliferate wildly and grow quickly. But they are hardy; perhaps the hardiest. And their beauty is truly sublime. I will come up just short of proclaiming them the most beautiful rainbow, but they are in the conversation. And after everything they've been through, the McCloud River between Lake Shasta and the McCloud Reservoir still holds genetically pure, native fish. There are also some big brown trout that have found their way up from Shasta, kokanee in the lower stretches in the fall and the occasional stray hatchery fish from the lake, but the vast majority of those forty or so miles has native rainbows only. The river also once was home to native Dolly Varden, but we screwed the pooch on that one too.

Enough about the fish for now. The river and her canyon are what really compelled me to figure out the fishing part. It's one of those classic deep, forbidding places. Almost every step is an adventure. While there are now sporadic trails etched along her banks, for the most part once you're fishing, you're in it and working pretty hard. And to properly fish the river, you have to move around. So it is a physically demanding one. And there are snakes. The bad ones. Lots of them, actually. Once down in the canyon around Ah-Di-Nah you are quite remote, so the sense of vulnerability is powerful. When you stop to think about where you are and what you're doing, the reality of your utter insignificance can weigh heavily. This is not a place where it is advisable to venture deep into the canyon solo. That occurred to me often on my early trips in there. But once Satchel joined, I never felt alone.

The river water is also something that needs to be seen. I've never beheld anything like it. From the deep springs on the shoulders of Mount Shasta, a dormant fourteen thousand-foot volcano, she comes to life, rich with minerals and middle-earth cold, and then descends slowly at first, gathering momentum and more water along the way. Mount Shasta's run-off contributes volume as well. After a series of spectacular falls, she meanders through the Hearst Property before finding the McCloud Reservoir. That stretch is commonly referred to as the Upper McCloud. There are many smaller springs, which continually feed into her up there. The aforementioned Hearst Property is a strictly off-limits area. And while I could never condone sneaking in there, I think you should totally do it if you ever have a chance. The fishing is off the hook! I had a Grey Drake day down there once that I'll never forget. Super illegal. But hell, man, she beckoned and I responded. So shoot me...

The river backs up in the reservoir and that is where you get your first real glimpse of the turquoise and emerald color. It's one of those colors that stop you in your tracks, as there's something about it that just doesn't register. But this is her, and how she'll be all the way to Lake Shasta. There are places in the river below the dam where you might have six to eight feet of visibility, but mostly it's less than that. That's her color, then there's the texture, the varying, infinitely complex feel of her flow. For the single-hand fly angler there is simply a little of everything. Whatever you may be seeking, she possesses. And with a typical summer flow between 150-200cfs, she's not a big one, but her bottom is one you don't want to mess with or allow apathy to set in while wading. So this is a river of many faces, incredible beauty, tangible danger and stunning fish. The complete package.

Interestingly, it was my friend and partner in far too many illicit and ill-founded endeavors to chronicle herein, Stefano, who first 'broke the code' on the McCloud. I had been back a few times over a couple years with little actual fish fooling. She was playing very coy with me, this new and most captivating *other*, and I loved it. I'd usually head down the dirt road to get as far away as possible, but several trips were quickies to Ash Camp. I was busy on every visit exploring up and down her canyon, discovering countless swirling pools, boulder-strewn pockets, slick runs. The fern and Elephant Ear, the moss-covered house-sized boulders, the near vertical ridgelines. I would name stretches based on an eagle's nest, unique rock formation or piece of trash found riverside. The place had heaviness, and also a beauty that struck straight to my deepest place; a place I'd sheltered from this brand of adoration.

But no, I hadn't fooled many fish there, and none over eight or nine inches. And so it was Stefano, who on one mid-spring trek to the river, actually figured it out, or at least began to. He returned well-chuffed and full of excitement. He'd been to Ash Camp and fished the water just above the footbridge. Using a Light Cahill Bird's Nest under a small corky indicator he had fooled several spunky natives. This report was all it took for me to be heading there within days. This was the revelation I had awaited. It should be noted that this event transpired before the "digital age". There were no cellphones, no Internet, no Facebook. It was a time of having to figure stuff out on your own, or rely on guys in fly shops, and we've already concurred that they are not always the most helpful folk. Nope, back then it was just go, get there and sort it out. *That* is what Stefano finally did.

I camped at Ash Camp with a day and a half to fish. At first light I was up and making coffee, stringing a rod, sheathing myself in neoprene. I went straight in at the slot water above the footbridge and within a half hour was into my first proper McCloud River rainbow. I remember like it was yesterday the heavy thumping and exaggerated leaps of that fish; my Orvis HLS eight-foot-six four-weight, *Poetry*, forming a perfect half circle as I attempted to lead the fish into my palm. And this trout will forever be etched in my memory, just as it remains tattooed on the outside of my right hand. While the color has long since fallen from the tattoo, the fish's still explodes. I'd encountered my first sizable native McCloud River rainbow. The brute strength and tenacity I'd been warned of, but no one bothered to express to me just how beautiful they are. From the silver-white of the belly to the blue-green emerald back, the crimson lateral line and gill plate, and the tiny, perfectly triangular white tip on its fins. This first fish would go a little over a foot, if measured in the way of man. If its dimensions were declared in the spirit of an angler, it would register much larger. The date was May 3, in the year 1996. I was thirty-one years old. Had recently bought a house, a little over a year after producing my first child. It was my fifth foray to the McCloud. The morning was clear, warm and without wind. The fish ate a size sixteen Bird's Nest, unbeaded. I'd just experienced an undeniably transformative moment. Even now, as I write this on nearly the twentieth anniversary of that day, my pulse quickens at the recollection; such was her spell. And oh, had she found a new victim.

I will not herein go to great detail of every other trip, every beautiful fish, every hatch, every pounding storm, all the friends I took there, all the friends I made; that and more will be in the book I'll write someday dedicated solely to the McCloud. Ours would be a long, deep and impactful relationship. The metaphor would be stretched taut with this one. My affair with the McCloud would truly overshadow all others, rendering almost every element in my sphere insignificant at best, completely irrelevant at worst.

It is only fair to now simply acknowledge her importance on a few levels. It was on her banks I met a man who eventually allowed me my first experience as a fly-fishing guide. Teaching somebody how to fool a fish was not new to me, but being paid to do it surely was. And to have it be a stranger was cool too. I didn't know if I'd like it or be any good. I did and I was. It was when engulfed in the deepest, narrowest reaches of her canyon that some of my greatest revelations overtook me; the strength girded within me to make life-changing decisions, and I was taught to keep putting one foot in front of the other; to have conviction behind my choices and believe I was doing what needed to be done. It was also on her banks that Michelie, my second wife (and soul mate) and I expressed our unceasing, unbreakable love to each other. Our commitment became an amaranth there amongst the greenest green in the spring of 2003 with Satchel as our witness. None of this was spoken, mind you; it was evoked. On her banks I watched my son go from boy to man as he explored both the great canyon etched in the earth, as well as the one he possesses in his spirit; as he found courage, instinct and balance, with an appreciation for the power of nature. And it was in her teal currents I skinny-dipped with a stripper, but elaboration of that event will have to wait.

These are but a few of the transfigurations. In the near twenty-year affair we shared, you can probably imagine much was seen and felt out there. It was not all good. And for sure as the fly-fishing experience gathered popularity there were times when I wished for her to duplicate and allow me the one where the masses weren't. But I always knew of a place or two where I wouldn't be bothered. I learned from her also that the minute you think you've got it all figured out, is when you'll be shown exactly how much you're clueless about; one of the greatest life lessons ever.

For now though it has been nice to introduce you to the greatest love of them all, the most meaningful *other*, and still the most beautiful place I've ever been. I know she's still there and a little piece of her misses me. I've not visited in a couple years; such is the mysterious tidal movements of life. I know I'll go back someday. We will both have changed, she through the natural shifting of elements and of forest fires, drought and man, me of the more rapid human aging process. But it will be a reuniting, heralded with all the fanfare is her due. She will welcome me, perhaps her biggest admirer, with an affectionate embrace. And I will approach humble and eager. Then I'll stop all movement, all thought, all breathing and allow her song back into my heart, supinely.

Chapter 6

My Brawling Trollop

It's not easy getting to know someone really well, like intimately, without becoming exposed to their friends, sometimes family even. Such was the case as my deep and impactful relationship with the McCloud River eventually led to such an acquaintance, her far less beautiful, far more dangerous pal the Pit River. What I mean by acquaintance is that they spill into the same great, disturbing blemish that is Lake Shasta. But aside from running in the same circles, so to speak, these two could hardly be any less alike. While the McCloud has wadeable, semi user-friendly terrain, the Pit is all large, slick boulders, embedded in a ruthless, scorching canyon. What makes the wading all the more demanding is the off-color water, a product of the large, silty lakes formed behind each hideous dam that PG&E saw fit to erect through her canyon. The river is fed by two springs in the Fall River and Hat Creek, along with her own springs far east in the great Modoc Plateau. Were she undammed, she'd rip down that canyon all day every day, a torrent all the way to the Sacramento River near Redding. As it is, she's held up and released constantly through five large dams, solely to make power for air conditioning-dependent sloths in the Central Valley. And now that I write this, her shitty attitude is of no wonder. How would you behave if captures were constantly releasing you only to take you prisoner again? If every time you felt the slightest inkling of freedom, you knew in the back of your brain, in the tenderest region of your heart, that there was still a tether affixed your back? Yea, I'd be pissed off too. This is not an original story, I know. It is one told far too frequently. But in the Pit's case, she is more prone to exhibit her discomfort. She does so in the form of near-impossible wading, absorbing and transmitting furnace heat all summer, being perhaps the snakiest canyon I've known, and housing some of the nastiest trout you'll ever meet. Oh, there are tougher rivers to fish, but not many. When you put her in comparison with her gorgeous, enchanting pal, the McCloud, she's just lecherous and bawdy.

And I love every deplorable, ass-kicking inch or her.

My earlier explorations into her deep, seductive and evil canyon were wake-up calls for me as an angler and man. I was so intimidated, but still convinced I needed to make sacrifices, give of myself, earn her interest. Perhaps the closest life metaphor I can conjure is way back in the summer after eighth grade when my friend, Nicky Craw convinced me to call a girl I'd met the previous school year. Her name was Jenni Muldaur, daughter of Maria, she of "Midnight in the Oasis" fame. What, you don't remember that hit song? Well hell, it was only forty-something years ago. Anyway, Jenni was super cute, in a badass kind of way. People were put off by her attitude and not sure how to deal with the daughter of somebody so famous. I was one of those people. Throughout the school year, we'd pass in the hallway and I'd nod and smile an awkward 'hello', all bouncing, feathered hair and waving corduroy bellbottoms, braces aglow in the fluorescent light. She'd stroll passed, rabbit tail-cute slightly upturned nose, perky new-boobs stiff in training bra, her painted on Jordache jeans, leaving precious little to the writhing, twelve-year-old imagination. And yes, I'm quite sure she smiled in return; just not in the traditional pushing back of one's cheeks kind of way. It was classic young love, blossoming in the sterile, wretched confines of middle school. At the time I was a football player, having already worked out with the nearby high school team, unwittingly preparing for what would become just another in a series of great lifetime letdowns. But I didn't know that at the time. I thought I was a stud, the next true local hero. And so when Nicky convinced me to call, it was with some positive intent mixed with ignorant bravado that I picked up the phone to do so. She had, after all written a loving passage in my yearbook, something along the lines of, 'Super cool getting to know you in music class this year. You totally shred on the recorder. Have a great summer and call me sometime, you know, if you want to, or whatever. Jenni'. And then she wrote her phone number. So we're over at Nicky's one afternoon and he talks me into actually calling. And she actually picked up. The conversation went something like this, only with each awkward pause lasting an eternity.

"Hello?" she said after perhaps the twelfth ring, by which time I was convinced there would be no answer, this being way back when there were no answering machines. So I was already pretty much screwed, all the resolve I'd mustered had evaporated at a trickle with each ring.

"Uh," was my debonair opening salvo.

"Who is this?" she snapped. It's occurring to me now that the Muldaur household must have received many calls from creeps trying to get through to the famous mom and Jenny was most likely the screener.

"Uh," I figured this the appropriate tact; just act pathetic, disoriented.

"I'm hanging up," she hissed.

"No! Don't!" Now I was really pouring on the calm, classy charm we middle school boys held in such spades.

"Yea buddy," she began, her words possessing the toughness she was known for. "I'm hanging up now,"

"It's Griff!" I belched, perhaps having the gumption to believe such a declaration would save me from the ringtone I would pretend to Nicky wasn't there as I continued a make-believe conversation with a dead phone line. And yet somehow it worked. Sort of.

"Ooooooookaayyy," she said, part in recognition, part no doubt wondering what the hell I could possibly want.

"Yea, hey, how's it goin'?" I stammered, somehow able to string a sentence together.

"Good." Her voice was now level-tone, unmoved.

"Good!" I parroted. "You?"

"Good," she repeated in a soft, tired-sounding sigh.

"NICE!" then I chuckled like a psilocybin-laced monkey. This was not going well at all. Her demeanor had me well and truly on my heels, and there would be no swift recovery.

"What's going on, Griff," she asked, with maybe just a little worry mixed with the trepidation.

"Yea, you know," I began, full of sudden, but fleeting verve. "I was just hanging out with Nicky and thought I'd call," and with that I lost all momentum.

"Thanks," was all she said, but that one word spoke volumes. She was ready to get back to whatever I had interrupted.

And then it just happened. I don't know how or why. I wanted to retrieve the words the second they slid from my mouth, writhing like a hatchery fish, banked, having fallen for chartreuse Powerbait. "You wanna go out sometime?" the words hung listlessly out in the ether for a desperate three or four seconds, without response. Or maybe that *was* the response. "You know, like to a movie or something?" And there followed another horrific delay, one I could no longer endure. "Jenni?" I'm quite sure the tone was beyond plaintive.

"No," was her answer.

Then the line went dead.

One word. One word that shaped every interaction with every girl for the next several decades. One word that created a young man devoid of self worth, gumption, a workable angle. From that day on, I was a snake in the grass. Abandoned was any style, any proper etiquette. From that one word rebuke arose a monster; a person I'm ashamed to admit was me. But a wily one I became; tenacious, biting at the ankles of any unwitting prey. Unwavering in my pursuit; just lacking the concept of proper preamble. And it was -and I suppose is- *this* guy who would approach angling many years later.

Why do I tell this story now? Well because the Pit River was the Jenni Muldaur to my barely pubescent angler persona. There I was, all humble, the pathetic blatherskite, effectively supine, possessing a small, lovely-scented bouquet in one hand, my sweat-stained fishing cap in the other, requesting only the humoring of my innocent need. And her laser-pointed rejection could not have more squarely hit my heart. In the Pit's case, I was allowed mere minutes in her swift, off-color currents before slipping and finding myself face down and afloat. The moment was a first for me as a fly fisherman. I'd slipped and fallen many times, but to be swimming, unable to locate bottom as water rushed into the gap in my waders the small of my back created was truly horrifying. I would regain my footing, obviously, but it would be sometime before I was remotely comfortable in her embrace again. I'd been spurned posthaste and thoroughly. She saw nothing in me worthy of her time. For her, as with Jenni all those years before, there was no charm in my innocence.

Months would pass before my next attempt. And with that effort came a new me. I'd conjured another angle, a method she'd find irresistible: I bought a wading staff. Yes, oh dear reader, this would be my salvation, my ticket to the holy land. Unwaveringly, I'd probe her every crevice. She would receive me devoid of refusal, guard down and arms-outstretched welcoming. And I was inspired.

Within an hour I was again swimming, the bent staff in one hand, the four-weight fly rod in the other, water once again slipping into the legs of my waders.

What I'd come to learn in the coming years was that her rejection of me and my desires was in no way unique. No, there was nothing special in her treatment of me. It was the same for practically everyone who dared ply her forbidden fruit. And I'd find that out only through much struggle, too many scary moments to recount, all the encounters with rattlesnakes, the endless bruised shins and involuntary swims. She would finally find it in her granite heart to allow me in and I'd get to know her completely. And she me.

I left it all in her canyon. For a solid decade she was a stop on almost every trek through "Trout Country", the part of California home to the Upper Sacramento, McCloud, Pit and Fall Rivers as well as Hat Creek and several insanely good lakes. I'd eventually fish and guide all of it, but in those early years of exploration I found myself increasingly drawn to the Pit's searing heat, demanding wading, secluded, unimproved campsites, and absolutely brutal fish. All her trout are wild. The bigger ones are football-shaped, big-shouldered beasts. They live in small "pillows" found in front of and behind rocks. The most effective method throughout the day is high-stick nymphing without a strike indicator. Put on a bunch of weight and wade to your spots, picking and poking at each likely lie. The Pit is where I first experimented with a Tenkara rod. But worry not, dear reader, it was short and unfulfilling experiment, leaving me feeling cheap and slightly soiled.

There were many, many memorable days there. One was recounted in my first book. That was the day I landed my first big brown trout in her baking, listless canyon. But the one I'd like to tell now was perhaps one of the most amazing days I ever spent waving a fly rod, and some of the glory was because of the fishing

It was in the early fall one year. I'd decided to take a trip back to my old haunts, revisit earlier mistresses. The 'Bou and the Middle

Fork were the plan. Spend a couple days on each. Rekindle romances practically forgotten in my new phase as trout bum, when only the McCloud, Upper Sacramento and Pit Rivers had compelled me. It was a trip much anticipated and prepared for. Yes, back to my old flames I'd venture, a more seasoned and accomplished angler, returning to display all I'd learned, but also a humble attempt at reconstituting long-buried lust.

At the 'Bou I found a choked in, barely recognizable iteration of the love I'd known. She had been starved of water and her banks were a tangle of shrub and weeds. Her low flow offered no romance. From the dam to the confluence she was an unalluring, depressing mess. I still wadered up and fished here and there, but it was a sad reunion to be sure.

That afternoon I drove up to the Middle Fork and set up camp. In the evening, I hiked into the canyon where so many spirits lived, so many fond memories endured. And yet at each pool, each run of boulder water, each once-was pocket, there were no fish. The pattern of flood and drought had rendered her a vague, pathetic version of the river I'd known. That night, sitting by the campfire, I mourned the loss of these great escapes I once so adored. I questioned whether the change has been more in me than them. I cursed anything I could hold responsible for their demise. And I wondered if the beauty I'd once seen in them was as profound as I remembered.

In the morning I broke camp and drove sadly out of the canyon. At some point I decided to go explore a new place, a creek which flowed out of a small reservoir only twenty miles from a nearby town. On my map it looked big enough to hold trout and I'd heard that the fishing might be worth checking out. What I found was a hideous irrigation ditch running along a road used primarily by trailer-towing trucks to and from the lake. I stopped here and there and tried to imagine what the fishing would be like if I were to actually try. In the end, I passed completely and began heading back towards town.

On the drive out, whilst distracted momentarily from the road ahead, a deer lunged into the roadway in front of me. At the speed I was travelling, there would be no swerving to avoid. The impact still haunts me today. I did manage to not hit it square on, but with the right front corner of the 4-Runner I'd bought a year or two before. It was a sickening thump, one that sent the animal ricocheting off the 'roo guard back towards the forest from which it had emerged. I slowed to a stop a couple hundred feet down the road and pounded the steering wheel, as if hitting the deer had been its fault. Part of me wanted to pull back out and drive on. But the bigger part needed to confront what I'd done. And so I switched off the motor and got out. It seemed a long walk back to the deer. I found it in a ditch next to the road. And it was alive. She was on her side, almost as it preparing for a nap. Her head and neck would have shown no evidence of her wounds. But it was her eyes that will forever stay with me. She had surrendered to her fate, that much was plain to see. And so there was a finality in her gaze. She knew, on some level, that her breaths were numbered. I don't know if she recognized me as the driver of the car that had delivered the blow. But as I knelt in close, she spoke in her soft gaze. Her heavy eyelids couldn't shield the beauty she possessed. And in that beauty there was an acceptance of her fate. There was also a forgiveness that made me weep as I talked to her. "I'm so sorry," I sobbed, no more than two feet separating us. "I didn't see you till it was too late." I wanted to cradle her, be there as she let go. But I couldn't bring myself that close. I was too ashamed, too scared of what that would feel like. And then I couldn't look at her anymore. My tears were embarrassing. What I'd done, through abject carelessness was inexcusable. That this beautiful, wild, harmless animal would die because of me was too much. And no, I don't buy the argument that the animal was stupid for running in front of me. Is it any less stupid to carve a swath out of a forest, pave it over and expect there to not be confrontations with wildlife that have called said forest home for millennia? I stood and regained composure enough to again apologize and wish her well as this life transitions to the next.

In town I stopped in the small general store and approached the clerk, a woman in her fifties wearing a tank top and the reek of stale cigarettes. I explained what had happened and that I couldn't bring myself to attempt any fashion of putting the deer out of its misery. She expressed sympathy for how I felt and assured me that mine was not an unheard of scenario in those parts. She would make a phone call and have someone go out and check on the deer. They would do what was necessary and I shouldn't worry any further.

As I drove westward, with no particular destination in mind, I came upon an intersection where if I turned right I'd be heading north, towards "Trout Country" some four hours away, or I could keep going straight and be home in about the same time. With my left forefinger I flicked the indicator switch up, and hung a right.

The drive north on 89 was full of deep sighs and a heavy heart. I couldn't shake the image of the deer's eyes. And I kept imagining beasts jumping out from the forest towards the road. Would the next one end my life as retribution? I drove far more slowly than I normally would. Through Lassen National Park I began to feel tired. It was only four or five in the afternoon, but the crappy nights sleep, the hours of driving over a couple days and the emotional exhaustion had all conspired to wipe me out. I pulled over and went for a short walk to the banks of Manzanita Lake near the west entrance to the park. For those of you unfamiliar, this lake is a "Special Trout Water" as they're referred to in California, meaning it is catch and release, single barbless hook stuff, full of big fish. Call me crazy, but there might be something to that regulation. So I strolled out to a little beach from where one can wade and, lo and behold, there were some of these giant trout rolling around. So back to the Tonka Truck-looking 4-Runner death machine and quickly into waders and boots. Once in the cold, clear lake I began casting a little caddis emerger out amongst the rising fish. Mt. Lassen, the great volcano, shone in late-afternoon sunlight. There wasn't a breath of wind. The cool from the lake crept into my waders, and for the first time in several hours I was left alone from the tormenting vision of the deer's eyes. I forgot momentarily the heartache. And began to really fish. Perhaps, in the grandest scheme of things, this solitary focus required to fly fish is what has drawn me so powerfully to it for so many years. Even lake fishing, with a small fly practically motionless sixty feet out on glassy water, demands an attention that filters most everything else out, good and bad. And so I centered my energy out there, willing a fish to see my fly. It would be perhaps fifteen minutes before contact was made. The little fly, having sunken to the right depth only a few inches under the surface, was swirled into the mouth of a rainbow that would push two-feet long. I set the hook as softly as I could and then held on for dear life as the fish bolted for the middle of the shallow, weedy lake. *Heidi*, the bamboo rod, bent cork to tip. The little CFO reel wheezed under the duress. Somehow the tippet and knots held for the first frantic moments. Then the tug of war commenced. Those who have battled steelhead understand this sensation. The fish was so far away and yet its power and tenacity was transmitted through all the line, the rod, down my arm and straight into my soul. Every headshake, roll and run was breath stealing. The thought of being only barely in control overwhelmed conscious action. And way out there the otherwise calm surface erupted. The fish sailed clear of the lake and came down with a massive splash heard from one shoreline to the other. All other anglers peered in the direction of the commotion. And for that first moment, only I knew that the fish was off. Then the long process of replacing backing and fly line to reel began. I started easing away to the lake's edge as I reeled, knowing that I still had many miles till a campsite. I'd achieved all that was needed just then. And it really had very little to do with fishing.

It was dark before I turned off Highway 89 and headed towards Lake Britton and the dam under which the Pit River assumes the guise she'll wear, for better or worse, all the way to Lake Shasta. This first area behind the dam is known as Pit Three. It is where I first came to know her. In the daylight, from the dam you look a mile straight down a river canyon. The entire stretch is full of large, exposed boulders and choked in tight on both sides with alder, oak and ash. The thick tuft grasses protrude from every viable crevice in the rock. It is, even from above and at some distance, a nasty, threatening place. On this night though, I drove over the dam in the dark night without stopping to peer into the dark throat of the dark-hearted canyon, and then down the road to the first campsite I knew. Rock Creek is a lovely little babbler that tumbles out of a steep hillside and into the Pit. The site is little more than a pull out, but it serves me just fine. A quick fire was made and cooked over. A few beers were downed, and then sleep overcame me. Precious little time was spent thinking about the deer that night. My fishing session had somehow put her to rest in my psyche. Little by little I had forgiven myself, which came through the tortured visions from my drive and the time spent staring and pine reflections atop Manzanita Lake.

In the morning, as I made coffee and cleaned a few things around camp, I picked up an empty beer bottle. Just before depositing it in my trash I noticed something on the rim. It was a little mayfly. A Blue-Winged Olive perched there, perhaps enjoying a little leftover Sierra Nevada Pale Ale. I looked close at every aspect of the perfect fly. I've always loved that bug. I know some hatches have flies three or four times the size and come off in larger numbers. But the Blue-Winged Olive represents something to me. It is the transitioning of the season, the turning of a page; something has been done, and there is still much more to do. So as I inspected the fly I smiled as sunlight crept down the canyon walls to my camp.

I set the vise up on my flimsy roll-top camping table and began pulling material for some little humpback Pheasant Tails. I had a ton of workable little dries, but my smaller nymph selection was unacceptable. The PT is a fun one to tie. I have a slight variation in mine, but the fly still only takes a couple minutes to complete once all the materials are composed. Knowing there would be flies lost in the river, I ended up with a dozen and half freshly spun bugs before breaking down the vise. A buddy pulled in and stopped on his way down to Pit Four with clients and told me the fishing had been slow. From the looks of the guys he was working with, I didn't put much in his report. The people who do well on that river have a certain look to them, a 'Let's get after this!' attitude. Those guys didn't have it, and certainly not in their rental Chrysler Sebring convertible, looking for all the world as if attending a Gay Dentist's Convention. Not that there's anything wrong with being gay. Or a dentist. Or driving a Sebring convertible. Or attending a Gay Dentist's Convention in a Sebring convertible. It's just a little conspicuous in the depths of the Pit River canyon.

So anyway, armed with freshly tied bugs I ventured towards the river, bamboo in one hand, staff in the other. By this point in our affair, I never entered her waters without the staff. From the moment I began fishing till I packed to leave, whether for a few hours or four days, the staff was unsheathed and at the ready. Little by little over the years the river and I had found a balance, a truce. Ours was that particularly volatile relationship. Almost adversarial. Undoubtedly, there was more I disliked in her than I liked. But the parts I did appreciate far outweighed the rest. In other words, her attributes allowed me to overlook her wretchedness. We've all encountered this one. You know, looks great from behind but tough to gaze upon from any other angle. Outstanding figure with awful teeth. Killer in the sack but can't complete a sentence. Brilliantly hilarious but you'd be afraid to introduce to close friends. I could go on...

You get the idea; it was a love/hate deal with equally potent forces imbedded in each. With the Pit, the handing of the baton from adoration to abhorrence and back again might occur hourly. But on this day in question a strange feeling came over me once in waders and aside her waters. For the first time I felt her welcome me, open armed and almost gently. Did she know what I'd been through? Did she know that just for this one day I needed a bosom to rest my troubled head upon? From my revisiting old flames only to find them denigrated by time, man and nature, to the hideous, stomach wrenching pain at having hit the deer, this had been a spiritually deflating trip. Now, as the sun shone on the Pit's vaguely turquoise, dancing currents, I felt home. My new home. Where I was supposed to be.

Into the braided water where Rock Creek enters. Feeling the bottom with my collapsible antennae, looking for that first seam to probe. The bamboo was equipped with a special custom leader Jan Kurahara taught me to construct. Without much detail, it had several small stretches of brightly colored Amnesia with the outer shell of floating fly line slipped over the blood knots basically acting as strike indicators as well as depth finders. As geeky as that all sounds, the design was super effective. Then the rig had an anchor knot a foot or so above the first fly. The knot was there to stabilize the three or four AB split shot applied in order to get my offering into the fish's house. This was not dainty business. My hard-fisted mistress would not humor the feathery touch required for a spring creek. She had no interest in what might endear on the McCloud. She wanted a pounding. And a pounding is what she'd get.

I found my footing mid-current and loosed flies from rod in preparation of the first cast. There were two of them; a Cahill Bird's Nest, beaded in a size sixteen and a fresh-from-the-oven humpback Pheasant Tail sized eighteen. Both were affixed 4X tippet. They were perhaps eleven inches apart; both for some reason filled me with a great sense of promise. I'd not been to the river in months, but as I stood there testing the knots, scanning up river and down, from its turbulent surface and up the thousand feet of pine and fir forest to the ridgeline and then straight above into the cloudless sky, I felt nothing but love, a swelling in my chest accompanied by a slight, intoxicated dizziness.

Then I made the first cast. The rig lobbed into the still morning air and alighted with a plop. The weight of the bamboo felt tremendous as I slowly lifted it into a high-stick position. I could feel the split shot depositing the flies to the bottom. The rig scraped over one boulder and then began dropping in behind it. What occurred in my psyche just then was the river equivalent to that moment when eyes meet across a smoky, crowded room. There's an energy transmission, as vague as it is unquestionable; this will end with crumpled clothing strewn in unfamiliar locations, bed sheets all but ruined, furniture deformed, bodies entwined, entangled, not fully understanding where one ends and the other begins. All having begun with the meeting of eyes. That's the energy I felt as the flies fell off the back of the first boulder. And then it happened. The tug was sharp, immediate. I barely needed to set the hook. The fish was already charging from its lie. The two feet of line hanging between reel and finger leapt through the guides and the reel buzzed angrily. The fish charged downstream and into the pocket below. There would be no obsequious following. I'd hold station and brawl. She had thrown me to the floor. Our first luscious kiss and tender embrace quickly forgotten. Now I was supine, she atop me, strong arms pushing down my shoulders, her mouth forming a perfect, wanton "O", having her way entirely. Her eyes were closed, her back arched, her full weight upon me, exhibiting complete, delirious control. And I would struggle only to please her. I know it's what she wants. I will writhe, pull to resist hers, push when she does the same. It's a heaving, tangled mess. It is heavy breaths, lust commingling with fear, smiling longing into aggression. She had no desire for my submission. And so I stood firm, legs solidly wedged into an unseen bottom, the fine bamboo torqueing, glistening. Tippet knots being fully tested. Then the line streaked towards the surface and a rainbow exploded into the morning light, deforming, shedding water into a thousand tiny diamonds.

A minute later the fish lay calm in my hand. Its head draped one way, its tail the other. It would measure fifteen or sixteen inches and weigh at least two pounds. The thing was practically oval shaped, nearly blue if you held it under the sun and sky just so. As with most of the rainbow trout in the Pit this one was almost obscenely thick-bellied. Its head looked too small for its body. The Pheasant Tail fell easily from its upper lip. And the fish slid back to the murky current from whence it had come.

I won't recount every fish caught that day. In truth there were too many to remember in detail. At one point two Pheasant Tails were affixed the rig, so effective the fly was that day. In my journal it was written, "at least twenty-five fish were landed between fourteen and eighteen inches". By early afternoon I was to be found atop a granite boulder the size of a VW Bug enjoying a smoke break. There were fall colors trembling in a soft breeze. Not another soul had intruded all day. There was a part of me as satisfied and spent as I've ever been on a river. I laid back and sighed deeply. I had returned to where I belonged. She welcomed me as only she can. In that moment

I felt used. I felt had, taken, yet triumphant, and still knowing completely that she wasn't done with me. Not even close, my brawling trollop.

Chapter 7

When First I Saw Her Face

Do you have the strength of recollection to peer back upon the moment you first saw your greatest love? Can you block out all of what may convolute, and the visions your conscious might compel you to *believe* is really it, and accept the truth? Because this object might not be what you think it is. And it might not be what you think it *should* be. Take a moment; as long as you need...

    I'm fascinated by what you may have just seen.

As I've documented herein, my life as an angler has been a series of heart-swelling encounters with rivers and trout. But there have also been numerous duds, too many ill-founded first dates to chronicle. Oh, I find beauty in most everything; that's not the problem. My bar is not unrealistically high. If anything, as my angler's path unfolded, I had brief and sometimes intense moments with *others* I'd rather not admit to. If it had a pulse, I was in. It wasn't a guilty pleasure because there was no guilt. She was there, I was there, and we got it on. Her, with currents sweeping around me, pushing, pulling, caressing, challenging balance and perception. Me, donned in Seal-Dry waders poised, not with a bouquet of wild, full-scented flowers, but instead a crappy four-piece Cortland fly rod, wanting only a glimpse of her essence; no intention stealing from her jewels; wishing her flow and mine might entwine momentarily. I would take nothing but a tactile memory.

    The Cimarron River in New Mexico is a classic example. Many years ago, while travelling with my first wife, Theresa, we stumbled upon this river. We were not on a fishing trip, but back then I never left the house without rod and a vest. We had ventured north from Santé Fe and sampled the Rio Pueblo flowing out of Taos full of eager cutthroat. That night we drove up and around the Enchanted Circle and spent the night in some windswept hellhole of a town. In the morning we made the short detour to see the Cimarron, knowing almost nothing about it. What we found there was an easily accessible, friendly little river just overflowing with brown trout. With the old trusty Double Hackle Deceiver, a fly developed on the 'Bou, I must have fooled thirty nice fish in a few hours while Theresa read in the spring sunshine. And as we drove away that afternoon, upon reflection of the morning we'd shared, I thought that I had, quite organically, encountered something amazing, been treated to orgasmically fun fishing, experienced all she could offer -even on her best day- and that as grateful as I was for the experience, I would never need to see her again. We had enjoyed our time together as much as we ever would. The universe saw to it that we would meet right then, satiate a curiosity, and be done with it.

I had many such encounters, both in my home state of California and also while travelling for fun or for fishing. And my adoration was no lesser or greater for them than for rivers I ended up acquiring a much deeper relationship with. They were quickies; meaningful, delicious, fulfilling, and brief by nature. But my heart, my spirit craved another level of connection, and that required complexity and challenge, character traits discovered in spades on the McCloud River in Northern California.

A handful of years ago, once my son Jasper had finished high school, the door swung open for Michelie, my current wife and I to get out of the area where I'd lived pretty much my entire life. She and I had shared a home for ten years there, co-parenting Jasper with his mom who lived a few miles away. For years we'd planned our escape. Marin County had changed drastically over time and had finally become, for me at least, unlivable. We were prompted to explore Central Oregon in search of a place to re-settle with our newborn daughter, Lola. The town of Bend back then was still quite depressed, not having recovered from the housing and financial crash of 2008. But even with the crappy job market and depressed economy, we fell pretty hard for a town with a river whispering through its heart. That trip was made in late-April. I'd driven up with the dog and camping gear, planning on sticking around after my girls and in-laws flew home. We got a hotel downtown and explored for a few days. We looked at various neighborhoods, ate at some good restaurants, played along the river and basically tried to imagine actually *living* in this amazing town.

I stayed in Bend after they'd left and camped just outside town. For the next week, I roamed freely, spending my days looking for job prospects, houses to rent, the occasional gullible trout and meeting people along the way. In the end, I found us a house and went back to Cali to begin the process of actually moving out of the one we'd been in for ten years. A week later, I learned that the corrupt property management company had given the house to someone else. So I planned another trip up the week after Memorial Day.

I actually drove north that Monday, figuring the traffic would all be heading back into the Bay Area and I might have a mellow drive up, even stopping for a quick fish on the Upper Sacramento. A couple hours into drive, a Giants game keeping me company and Eddy dozing in the back, I realized that I'd left my fishing chest pack and backpack in the house. So thorough was I in organizing my gear that it had all come into the living room for a proper tinkering with. And that is where my packs were left. After a quick call to Michelie to confirm my screw up, I quickly surmised that I was hosed. The bag with waders, boots, etc. was in the car, as were a couple rods and reels. But the flies, tippet, nippers, forceps, extra fly boxes, et al were at home. And there would be no turning back for them. So I bit the bullet and went into my least favorite fly shop in this or any other land, The Fly Shop in Redding to score a few flies. The guys were as unhelpful and heartless as I'd come to expect, but I still bought a couple spools of tippet and some big bugs for the Upper Sac.

My session there that afternoon was fun; a personal "One-Fly Contest". Some nice bows were fooled at one of my sweet little unknown zones, all falling for the large Stimulator, and then I was back on the road just before dark. Knowing I still had the better part of five hours till my campsite, my biggest error of the entire trip up was stopping in Weed for the Asian BBQ across from the Chevron station. As tasty as the grub was, food coma set in a mere hour later. The last several hours of the drive were as dozy as I've ever endured. Windows open, talk radio cranked, a handful of smokes and nothing but a slit in the forest, black, devoid of life or other motorists, minutes feeling like hours, eyelids drooping heavily.

I camped again down at Tumalo State Park and spent another week hanging out in town. I had made the acquaintance of Tye, the manager of the fly-fishing department at the big Orvis store in the mall. He and I share a mutual friend and had hit it off on my first trip. Upon arriving in town on trip two, he told me that the Salmonfly hatch was in full swing on the Lower Deschutes and I had to go fish it. I informed him that this trip was strictly business for me; that I had to find a house to rent and look for work because we had committed to moving. "Dude!!" he exclaimed, in what I would learn is classic Tye fashion, "It's Salmonfly! You HAVE to check it out." He excitedly led me to the fly bins and pulled out two of the stupidest looking things I'd ever seen. "This is it, dude. All you need. Just drive down to Mecca and fish it against the banks."

"I don't know, man. Not sure if I'll have the time. Really gotta get some stuff done while I'm here." With each word I could see the disappointment and dissatisfaction welling up in him. But, being Tye, he accepted my excuse, a little.

"Just take the flies, Duder. They're called Chubby Chernobyls. Remember the Chernobyl Ant? Well this is its big brother. Just slap it down hard along the banks. The take is crazy."

"Thanks, man. I'll do my best," was how I left it with him. The Chubbies went into my pocket and then the center council of the Outback, where they would remain for the next few days.

I was at a local pub late one afternoon, getting my grub and beer on while surfing Craigslist for rental house action, when Tye and some other guys walked in. We exchanged hellos. "So'd you get those Chubbies wet yet?" he asked with genuine enthusiasm.

"Nope. Not sure if I'm gonna have time."

"DUDE!!!" he began getting even more animated than before. "It's ON! Right now. It's only an hour away. Just go in the afternoon. It'll blow your mind."

"Okay, okay. I'll try to make it happen," I offered, not wanting to bum him out any further.

I went back to my computer and scheduled a few appointments for the next morning and then considered getting out to the river. The day after was already out, and the day after that I was heading home with a stop at the McCloud to meet my old pal, Scott for day of slapping Stimulators for some rainbows there.

I was done with seeing houses and on my way north on highway 97 around two in the afternoon. Once through Madras the road begins a steep descent into the big river's canyon. I was at once struck with the dramatic, near table-flat rim, the vertical basalt layers, the sense of enormity. I was reminded of the Grand Canyon, just on a much smaller scale. Before I ever saw the river, the pelting began. *Pop, pop, pop.* Was there a small army of delinquent kids stashed amongst the roadside brush armed with slingshots? *Pop, pop,* it continued. For me to suss out the source of the ambush, I had to refocus, slightly closer to the front of the car. Then I saw them. And then, once I realized what I was looking at, I saw many, many more.

There were flies -aquatic insects- crowding the air as I dropped in next to the river. The flies were approximately the size of my little finger. And there were thousands of them. No, millions. The attack on my windscreen continued as the road paralleled the river. I was on river-right and going with the flow. First impression: the river itself reminded me of the Lower Sacramento near Redding. It was, of course, much more beautiful, but then again shriveled, blackfly-covered dog turds are more attractive than the Lower Sac. I was having a hard time really looking at her though. The flies were just pelting the car, flying clumsily right into traffic like a great horde of locusts.

I pulled into the road that I was told would lead to Mecca Flat campground and immediately saw a sheriff standing beside his cruiser blocking the road. Then I saw another sheriff a hundred feet behind the first, leaning on his SUV. Then, I thought of the distinct reek of weed in the Subie. I came to a slow stop. The first sheriff, young, fit and obviously agitated began walking towards me. I shut the engine off and jumped out. We met midway between the two cars. Before I could even offer a greeting, he blurted out, voice breaking just a little, "You can't come in here!" Then there was an awkward silence as I peered over his shoulder at the much older, much more relaxed sheriff. Both their rigs were parked in the road, the same road I was to take to the spot where I'd slap my Chubby against the bank for the take of a lifetime. I re-focused on the young sheriff. He blurted on, still lacking any sheriff-like composure, "The road's closed!" I suppose he was expecting some kind of response, but I was in gotta-go-fishin' mode, and he was in my way. And so, in the vacuum that was my reaction, he went on, "It's a crime scene. You can't go down there." And then as if a terrible vision filled his brain, a vicious odor assaulted his every olfactory perception and he was fighting back vomiting, he said with as much effect as he could, "The road's *closed*!"

"Yea, that's what you said," I began, once again looking over his shoulder. "So how do I get down there to go fishin'? Can I just hike in?" His eyes grew big at the thought of anyone going down that road just then. "You see, I have a Chubby in my pocket," and with that I affixed his panicked eyes, then continued, "With the implicit instruction to slap it against the bank down at the campground."

Now we had a standoff on our hands. He sort of half squealed, "You can't go down there! It's a crime scene!" Desperation was setting in. Then he looked over his shoulder at the other sheriff, and beyond, down canyon, at the source of his nightmare. The older sheriff began approaching us. The younger guy turned back to me and tried to get a grip, "The road's closed," he said yet again, only this time almost level-toned. Then we stood in silence for five seconds until the older sheriff was there. He paused for a moment, kicking random rocks, scanning the canyon nonchalantly. Then, from a mouth that barely moved, with a soggy toothpick lodged beneath a un-trimmed, grey mustache, which was in turn under a set of seen-it-all eyes that were mounted under unmoving, bushy eyebrows, the entire countenance shielded from the late-spring sun by a crisp, tan Stetson, the words eased out, "The road's closed. Yer gonna have to go someplace else."

"Yea, that's what your pards was sayin'" I began, figuring if I went full hick we might relate. Then, in an almost whisper I went on, "You see, a buddy of mine down in Bend, nice guy that he is, gave me a big, golden-bodied Chubby. You wouldn't believe the size of this thing. Told me to slap it down along the bank at Mecca Flat." I scanned the eyebrows for movement. None. "Yup. Said that's all I needed to do. Claimed I wouldn't believe the explosion." The three of us stood, all within a few feet on the rutted dirt road, a slight breeze caressing the moment. The eyebrows hadn't budged but the toothpick had exchanged one piece of mustache shade for another. "So, there any way I might be able to get to the river down there?"

"The road's closed," he drawled. "Yer gonna have to find somewhere else to fish, friend." There was zero friendliness in his tone. And thus I accepted his word, spun and returned to the car. Before getting in I turned back to the Sheriffs. "You think you're gonna be here long," I asked

"Yea! For sure!" the young one yelped, nodding his head in a blur. The old guy agreed almost imperceptibly.

I drove across the road to a large parking lot next to the river and tried to figure out my next move. There was, at the moment, no plan "B". I'd learn this lot is the boat ramp for a stretch of the Lower Deschutes. But just then all I really wanted to know was where I could go and slap my Chubby. The bank on the far side looked good. As I stood, beer in one hand, smoke in the other, an old pick-up truck pulled in and parked. And middle-aged Hispanic guy hopped out and strode towards me while popping open a PBR. I nodded "hello" and turned back to face the river. When he was a few feet away he greeted me with, "How's it goin'? Guess we're not gettin' down to Mecca, eh?"

"Guess not. Sounds like they got some kind of crime scene down there."

"Yup. Them crazy Indians, man. Wonder what they did this time."

"Indians?" I had no idea what he was talking about.

"That's all tribal land on that side of the river. From the dam to the boundary twenty-five miles down," Just then a large trout ripped open the surface of the river against the far bank to pound a Salmonfly.

"Can I fish over there?"

"Nope." Then another big fish did the same thing twenty feet above the first.

"What would happen if I did?"

The guy shot me a "no bullshit" look and answered evenly, "You don't wanna know."

He invited himself to come stand close, leaning against the car with me. It was hard not to notice all the ink covering his upper body. He wore a "wife-beater", slightly sagging jeans and had a wallet chain looping to his back pocket. His facial hair was impeccably trimmed, hair slicked back, reflective lens Pilot glasses disguising any sense of expression. We stood kicking rocks for a long minute. Then he said, "I'm waiting for a buddy coming down from PDX. We were gonna camp at Mecca. Suppose we'll head down to Trout Creek."

Boy, did that have a nice ring to it. "Where's that?" I asked trying to not sound like a complete idiot.

"Oh, down river a piece. You can follow us down there if you want. He should be here soon."

I peered over my shoulder back at his truck. "Nice rig," I complimented.

"Thanks, man. Ground-up restoration all by myself. Sixty-four Chevy. Fuckin' love that thing."

"That's the year I was born," I told him and again took a long look at the truck. It appeared like a piece of art with the river and a few Poplar trees as the background.

A little while later his buddy showed up on a motorcycle with saddlebags overflowing with gear. After a brief discussion they agreed to head towards Trout Creek with me in tow. The drive was dramatic as we went back up the canyon and then across a broad expanse of alfalfa fields before dropping into and through the tiny town of Gateway. There, we turned off and headed west back towards the river. And it got remote. Now, I'm not the paranoid type, but at some point it occurred that we'd passed no signs indicating a "Trout Creek Campground" and that I was following strangers into completely unfamiliar territory after having just left the scene of an apparently grisly crime. But as I've done many, many times, I let the winds blow me toward whatever fate awaits. A cold beer was tucked between my legs, the day was unbelievably gorgeous, I was traversing roads at the end of which could be anything, nobody knew where I was, it was just the dog and myself. Reggae blared from the door speakers.

Then the road began a steep decent on rutted, wavy gravel. The guys pulled over and told me to go first. They would go slowly from there to the river. And so off I went. The rest of the road beyond the steep hill and railroad tunnel was bad, but the Subie did what she does and we soon found ourselves on the banks of the mighty Deschutes. The guys were a few minutes behind and I was already in waders by the time they showed up. They told me that they'd fish later.

The dog and I began walking downstream along a glassy, seam-addled run. The right side bank was crowded in with juniper and alder. And I *had* been told to find overhanging foliage and cast around it. The big bugs were everywhere, mating in the tall grass, flying clumsily over the river, clinging to branches. Every few minutes one would crawl onto the back of my neck, having worked its way up my waders and over my shirt. It was the largest insect I'd ever encountered on a river in such amazing numbers. And every minute or two one would fall to the river's surface and get clobbered by a trout.

Amazingly I had that stretch of river to myself. There was a guy a ways upstream on the far bank who had rowed over in a small canoe. He was fishing the reservation along a stretch where it is permitted so long as you possess a Tribal Permit. There were some fish rising out in the middle of the river where it looked like a boulder garden broke the surface a little. I was fishing a stout five-weight that allowed me to reach quite a ways out from a large boulder just above the small rapid where Trout Creek joins the big river. And there *I* was, against all the tips I'd been given, hurling sixty-feet of line out towards fish that were feeding on something other than Salmonflies. And I did this for a half hour. Then, upstream and under branch, there was a tremendous, heaving splash. I redirected my attention to an equally difficult cast. This presentation would require forty to fifty feet of sidearm chucked up under overhanging alder branches. From where I stood I could see several large flies affixed to some of them. The Chubby proved a challenge to move accurately on a long leader, but I made a bunch of tries nonetheless. After maybe five minutes of attempting this cast, I decided to try a shorter leader. While drawing the line in to make the change, the fly landed eight feet off the bank and maybe fifteen feet in front of me. What happened next stole my breath and etched an image in my head that has not fled. Out of perhaps eight feet of water a torpedo shot up and positively annihilated my big, golden-bodied Chubby. I'd never witnessed such an aggressive take, not for grasshoppers, October Caddis, big stones on the McCloud. Not ever. The fish's momentum carried it out of the water two feet as it took the fly. It was an eighteen-inch 'bow, fat and full of big-bug protein. Its next move was for the middle of the river posthaste. Out there it jumped several times. From my boulder I could only watch, slack-jawed and stunned. The next minute changed the way I think about dry fly fishing for trout. This fish was far larger and way, way nastier than my typical quarry. But its tenacity was what impressed most of all. The fish simply would not stop brawling. It had a repertoire of barrel rolls, somersaults, headshakes, reel-burning runs, savage darts for the bottom and heavy surface thrashing. Rarely have I ever just held on like that with a trout. Fortunately the hook was buried just so and I was able to get the fish to my hand. After a quick introduction I thanked the heavy Redband for having the grace in its heart to engage me. The fooling of that fish had nothing to do with skill; I'd just gotten lucky. Even though only a foot and a half long this fish would weigh over three pounds. Its dimensions were masculine, powerful and purpose-built. I cradled it for a moment before its release. Then, I set about getting another one.

And then five more after that.

Within a hundred yards of river I fooled a bunch more fish. Some took the Chubby the second it hit the water. Some took two or three swipes at it before either eating, or not. Some ate it when it sunk and began swinging at the very end of the drift. Every one I landed would be between sixteen and twenty inches. All super healthy and brutally strong. In the middle of the day, under a hot, bright sun, the fish were coming out of really deep water to smack the Chubby. The grab was easily one of the coolest things I'd ever witnessed on a trout river.

It was a session I'll never forget. For months afterwards I was certain that every trout in the Lower Deschutes was that size, and they all fought like crazy, and ate anything huge you threw at them. I'd learn, of course that the reality is far different. But as a first impression, she could hardly have been more enthralling.

I won't go into too much detail of what caused the road closure. It's easily found by researching "Rail Tunnel Beating". And from what I heard in the days immediately following, the young sheriff had every right to be shaken up.

Now I call the Lower Deschutes my office as well as my mistress, muse, siren and seductress. Over the last handful of seasons my time with her has increased, but there isn't even a hint of ennui creeping in. She has more faces than I can count, and even more moods. Her challenges are so vast and multi-layered that I'll be intrigued till my last day. She can be as giving or as stingy as any *other* I've known, sometimes in the same day. And she possesses unique, quirky regulations, meant to keep some of her secrets hidden forever. Little could I have known that first afternoon, when first I saw her face, what she would come to mean to me. Now I guide her over a hundred days every year and fun fish her for another thirty or forty.

The following stories were written over the 2014-2016 seasons. Many began their life as blog posts for the website at the fly shop I work for. I fleshed them out a bit in the months after they were first published. And now they're here, offering the reader a glimpse into the world of guiding and fishing the Lower Deschutes River, my most beloved, demanding *other*. The one I should have probably been with the whole time.

Chapter 8

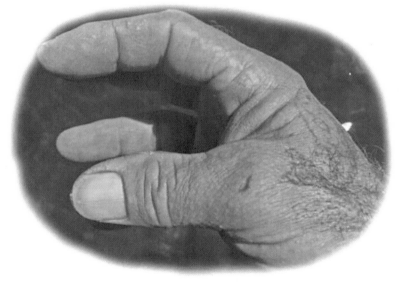

My Wife's Poor Nipples
Or
Summer on the Deschutes

Early Summer

Perhaps this is an inappropriate chapter title for a book such as this. Not that it's potentially offensive; there is simply no eloquence. It doesn't fit the narrative. It's unimaginative and coarse. Maybe if I just reversed it... But anyway, it's important, actually imperative, that you understand how much I love my wife's nipples. They are, to me, the eighth wonder. Since the day I met them, er, her, I've had the most deep fondness. And it's not just me. Their grandeur is appreciated far and wide. When we find ourselves strolling a busy sidewalk, other women will lose track of cellphone conversations, spilling their mocha Frappuccino upon an unwitting passersby, stumble into strangers at the distraction her nipples caused. It's a common and comical practice. And that's with *women*. Imagine how men react. They are known to mow over hapless leashed pets, chest-bump parking meters, diminish the partner they're with just to take in the beauty and perfection. Right now, at a little before five in the morning, they're up there, in our bed, protruding just a little, the most perfect, delicious thing ever. I really am quite fond of them, would never intentionally bring them discomfort. My sole interest is to admire and adore, and occasionally fondle.

And then here comes summer. I'm on the river more days than not, grinding out eight-hour guide trips day after day and my hands go all to hell. This is Central Oregon after all. It's either muddy or dusty. Very little in between. The canyon of the Lower Deschutes is an especially dry and inhospitable place. All day long there is wear and tear on my hands. Nothing I do helps, no amount of lotion, salve or ointment. The callouses develop and don't go away. Flesh dries and splits around fingernails. The skin on the back is an obscene, wrinkled, worn-leather brown. The palms are rough, riddled with ruptured blisters, cuts of varied size and depth. They are quite simply a hideous mess. Literally two days ago I went downtown to pick up Michelie and Lola at a manicurist shop and half jokingly showed my hands to the lady there while posing the question, "Could you do anything with these?" She briefly peered down at the worn and dying hide that has become my hands and recoiled abruptly, looking momentarily as if she might vomit, covering her mouth, closing her eyes, her head shaking jerkily side to side, trying to erase the vision. I took that as a 'no'.

It's been a long couple months for me. Starting back in April I began running three-day trips from Trout Creek to Maupin on the Lower Deschutes. We had incredible weather and fishing. Those trips are brutal on the hands because it's day after day, constant exposure, setting up and breaking camps, rowing many hours, hauling anchors and fishing hard. Mid-April saw me hosting a three-day educational program down at Lake in the Dunes near Summer Lake. This is an annual event that has grown in popularity and is one of my favorite things we do at Fly and Field Outfitters. This year we had twenty-something people down there. The weather was off the charts perfect. Each day was sunny, relatively calm (a true rarity) and the fishing was silly good. The only downside to the three-plus days I was there is that Lake in the Dunes is basically in an old, dried up lakebed. And that lake, when it contained water, was very high in alkaline and salt. The loose dust is everywhere and just sucks the moisture out of skin. This was how my season began. Then it was back down for a series of five multi-day trips during the famed Salmonfly hatch. A couple of these were back-to-back, meaning six straight days of abuse. By the end of May, my hands were completely toast, repulsive, filthy, rough paws barely fit for the steering wheel of my truck, let alone something as worshipable as my wife's perfect nipples.

When you're on the river as much as I've been, that means you've been away from home and all its comforts. You know, a soft bed, the occasional shower, time with my kids. That kind of stuff. There are other things that especially appeal when home, even if only for one night. And one of those things, for me, is playing with my wife's nipples. Sorry, there's just no other way to say it. Not intending to offend. And to her credit, she humors my attention, regardless of the obvious discomfort. It's a fragile balance we keep. She deserves the very highest marks.

I'm quite sure you didn't buy this book to read about my wife's nipples, although I'd hardly blame you if you had. They are really quite marvelous. So perky. Prettier than a rose and way more fun to play with. No, you must have picked up this here book for some fishin' stories.

And so here you go.

Damn, I can't think of one right now. Distracted...

Okay, got one. I had a day off back in late April. My son, Jasper was in town. I had a hunch there might be a stretch of the

Middle Deschutes with a few big bugs so we set off early one morning and parked up on the canyon rim. The part of the canyon we were trekking into is one I've wondered about for years but never dared try. Jasper was game for an exploratory effort and so off we went armed with a backpack full of beer, some munchies and rain jackets, just in case. The hike down was the easy part and soon we were drowning big nymph rigs in the deep, hydraulic runs. We each fooled a nice fish or two before losing the flies in the crusty, lava bottom. I had seen a couple Salmonflies in the grass along the river and on a whim tied on a medium-sized golden-bodied Chubby Chernobyl, mostly because I was feeling too lazy to re-rig the nymphs. Out in the middle of the run there was a big boulder I had purposefully avoided under the bobber, but with the big fly it looked really good. Jasper had come up and was putting another nymph rig on when I made the first cast with the Chubby. The fly splatted down, drifted eight feet to the rock and a chunky brown trout charged out of at least six feet of water to crush it. The take was my first Chubby grab of the season. Every year we psyche ourselves up for the big bug and the insane behavior of the fish when it's around. And every year the first time a fish eats our obnoxious imitation it's giggle-inducing. This event was no exception. As the fished charged around the run in front of us, I chuckled like I'd stolen something.

What followed was one of the most amazing days of slapping Chubby I've ever had. I was using my eight-foot five-weight bamboo rod, *Heidi*, having just gotten a new tip sent up from the builder in California. It had a slight separation in the strips of wood and I'd sent it down to him almost a year earlier. I don't use that rod up here as often as I did in California. I've just seen too many bad situations with rods breaking, and most of the time I'm in my drift boat anyway. Bamboo and drift boats don't go together so well. The rod was behaving brilliantly, chucking the big bug with plenty of authority but still offering that near-orgasmic sensation when playing a solid trout.

Jasper quickly changed to a big dry and began crushing it. At one spot where a stretch of broken water tumbles into the next run, on a seam of current no more than five feet off the bank, he hooked six fish on eight casts. I watched it all from a rock above and every take was as cool as the others. The fish lose all inhibition as they rip towards the fly. Several of them launched clear of the surface simply because of their momentum, their eagerness to eat it. None of these fish were huge, but anytime you have fourteen to sixteen inch brown trout charging the big bug, you're having fun. And to be there with Jasper for his first proper day of slapping Chubby for browns was as good as it gets.

The day went on at a pace I can only refer to as delirious. There was no rush but we also had much ground to cover. Having never been up that area, I kept us moving just enough to have the sense that we were making solid progress. The canyon down there is a harsh and foreboding place. The rocks are all quite large and spaced in such a way to make getting around really taxing. I had scouted the canyon from above a couple times and knew it would be tough. Once actually down in it, the true difficulty of the place emerged. From one run to the next there was crawling up and sliding down on huge basalt boulders. I don't recall one easy step the entire day.

Sometime early in the afternoon the clouds moved in and a light rain fell for an hour or so. The fishing was unaffected as the browns just kept rushing up to our flies. Sometimes we were casting to a fish we saw rise and sometimes just to likely spots. But more often than not something ate. When the rains started I was targeting an amazing ledge on the far side of a deep run. Several rocks jutted out creating micro back eddies and making the drift pretty tricky. A bunch of good presentations went by before the fish finally crushed the Chubby. But when it did I was tied into one of the bigger browns I've ever seen down there. What followed was a comical shit show of me trying to subdue the fish while really trying not to fall in the river. The rocks had gotten slick under the rain and I was flailing. Eventually the big trout found a ledge below me and tied the rig off nicely before breaking the fly from the tippet. The entire episode lasted maybe ninety seconds. I actually saw the fish swim off with the Chubby still in its mouth.

When the sun came back out, the fishing went to crap. Thankfully, we had made it to the upstream throat of the canyon and the trail out. The entire lap for the day would measure a couple miles but it was as hard as I've worked for it in a long time. And there's nobody I would rather have made that adventure with than Jasper. He'd had a day he'll never forget. The cold beer back at the truck was especially tasty. And on the drive home we shared our impressions of the day deep in the canyon, chuckling often. That's how any really good day of fishing should end.

I'd love to share more of my fishing exploits with you from the last couple months, but the sad truth is that I've done very little. What I have done quite a lot of is guide people into catching fish. And believe it or not, that has become every bit as rewarding and fun for me as catching my own. Some of you may scoff at that notion, or perhaps not even believe me. But it's true. I do love to fly fish. That will never die in me. But over these last bunch of seasons, guiding the local river systems, engaging people from all over the place with skill levels as varied as their backgrounds, fishing *through* the client has become every bit as cool for me as my own fishing time. Granted I have to maintain a certain level of professionalism with clients; I can't necessarily say and do everything I might were I out with buddies, but the experience of getting clients into fish rocks my world. And so in retracing my steps since April I have so many amazing memories.

The time leading up to the Salmonfly "hatch" was really fun on the Lower Deschutes. The crowds hadn't arrived yet but the fish were chowing on big nymph combinations every day. Almost. It was good to see the fish getting back to a proper protein source after the long winter of little stuff. And to be floating the canyon in less than four layers of clothing was especially nice. At one point in the middle of the month I had four days in a row on the "Day Stretch". The fishing report read something like this: Excellent-Crap-Excellent-Crap. Same flows. Same weather. Just the most remarkably flip-floppy fishing I've ever seen down there. The last day was spent with two beautiful women over from Portland. Rarely have I developed such a crush on a couple clients. But they were gorgeous, fun, hilarious and super focused on fishing. And we grinded. They both got on with the program from the first stop and I just couldn't get a fish to eat. At our first left side stop of the day, at a bucket that had produced all spring, Elizabeth finally hooked up with a beautiful Redband. She played it with the right balance of authority and tenderness until it folded into my net. Her appreciation for the moment, for the stunning, perfect fish, for the day with her friend far away from their norm, made her even hotter. That day, for as long and difficult as it was, sticks out for the simple reason that they didn't care about how many fish were caught; they just kept fishing. And laughing, and loving the canyon.

After that, things just sort of plodded along for a week and a half. I was busy on the "Day Stretch" as well as getting camp ready for the onslaught of multi-day trips beginning in May. The first of these was another "Shake-Down" float. This is when a handful of guides and shop employees head down the "Camp Stretch" with all the gear for our client camp and work out kinks, either repair or make a list of items that need it, go through every piece of the kitchen, plot camps for upcoming trips, and maybe, occasionally fish here and there. The first such trip back in early April had been a blast. Two of my river guides ran Whitehorse Rapid for the first time, one in my boat with me sitting in the front; not an experience for the feint of heart. The fishing on that trip was by all accounts as good as it gets down there under a bobber. Many, many times we had "doubles". There were stops that produced easily forty fish between two or three rods. The trout were just out and feeding freely, such was their early spring world down there, before we show up *en masse* to put hooks in their faces every day. The May trip was not as good, but we enjoyed gorgeous weather, uncrowded camps and we ran into the big bug day two. From somewhere below Whitehorse to the take-out day three we chucked Chubby and had as much fun as grown men are allowed. There were only four of us on that trip. The second night, after an epic day of chuckling like maniacs at each explosive grab, we didn't even fish around the camp, so sated were we.

Which brings me to the event that is Salmonfly. Not everyone has heard of this "hatch" on the Lower Deschutes. For that small handful of cave-dwelling monks, it is a "hatch" of biblical proportions, both in size and numbers. It will vary year to year, but every season since I've been here, the "hatch" has produced a lot of flies. The nymph begins its migration based on water temperature. Without getting too detailed, or leaping atop my soapbox to rant, this happens earlier in the calendar year nowadays, as we control-hungry men have seen to it to manipulate water temps by allowing water to flow from both the top and the bottom of the massive concrete abominations upriver. So the nymphal migration starts a bit earlier than it has in years past. This has thrown a wrench into the otherwise fairly predictable fishing patterns surrounding the "hatch". I put that word in quotes because like all big stoneflies the Salmonfly crawls to the bank to emerge. The dry-fly fishing, therefore, doesn't begin when that happens. That starts a few days later when the adult fly, you know, starts getting it on. Then they move into the grass and riverside trees. Then they either get all post-coital dopey or just grab a nap, loose their grip and fall in the water. I suppose this is as good a time as any to mention how large this fly is. It's big. I've seen them practically the size of my pinky. And I have a big, thick pinky, if you know what I mean. So this is a large fly. They have a prehistoric look to them, all segmented body, double helicopter wings, big eyes and super clingy, grabby legs. But they are not graceful fliers, and even more pathetic when on the surface of the river. Every season an accumulative bunch of time is spent watching one, having either fallen to the river or maybe, just maybe tossed in, and now it's drifting helplessly, wings struggling in vain to get oafish body aloft and you can almost hear it's little brain screaming, "Oh shit! Oh Shit! I'm gonna DIE!" Splash!

But back to what I beginning to explain: the dry fly fishing is best during a prolonged warm weather pattern and maybe the first day it cools off. The bug just doesn't really get active until the air is mid-seventies and they really go crazy if we get mid-eighties for a few consecutive days. When it cools off or gets rainy the bugs will hunker down in the base of the tuft grass and ball up to keep each other warm. That's when the snakes move in. Yea, *those* snakes. The ones that could rock in mariachi bands. They love the big bug too. As the nymph migration happens earlier in the year because of the manipulated water temps, the presence of adults bugs moves up too, into a time of the spring with less predictable weather patterns than even a couple weeks later, closer to the end of May and the beginning of June. So the fishing has grown a bit spottier. As our trips begin earlier, so does the potential for funky weather intruding. This year was no different. We had some truly epic trips through the middle of May, days when the Chubby fooled many fish, days spent giggling like schoolboys in possession of a naughty magazine. I spent hours standing high above clients who had worked down the bank after a rising fish or some likely water and watched great big, chunky, protein-laden Redbands launch from unseen lies to annihilate not-so-delicately placed Chubs; each grab as incredible to behold as the one before. These days are what has created the buzz around the "hatch". Then there were cool, windy periods when the dry fly fishing went to crap. Not much we could do about it. So back under the bobber we went. Fish were caught. We set up incredible camps. Cooked delicious meals. Rowed our asses off. We did everything we could do. But the big bug would be down and stay down until the weather improved.

There *was* one day... As many of you probably know, or have surmised based on the probably long-forgotten premise of this story -no, not my wife's poor nipples, the part about how it's either dusty here or muddy- every now and again it does rain in Central Oregon. And even less common is the proper downpour. Well, one of our multi-day trips began in one of those. We had four guys who had flown out from the east coast just to fish with us during the famed Salmonfly hatch. They had arrived the day before and would leave from the take-out ramp to fly home. And sure enough, they were greeted by a bucketing rainstorm for Day One of their trip. It was a day when I felt great pity for our "Bagger", the guy who rows all the gear straight to camp and sets everything up in preparation of our arrival in the evening. Ours was a morning of scrambling into waders in the Safeway parking lot before the clients even showed up; such was the severity of the storm. Martin, the other guide and I were already soaking wet. Down at the ramp we waited for the small porch on the old River Keeper's shack to come available for the crew to wader up and fill dry bags. The ramp itself was a carnival of guide boats, "bagger" rafts, and recreational folks heading down in anything that floated. I'd never seen anything like it. And I just wanted to go home. I could only imagine the big bugs down there huddled up in the grass, the fish taking a "digestion" day and the fishing simply sucking. Once our boats were in the river, I went about getting the keys for our "bagger" and the client rig into my truck with instructions as to where they should end up, and Martin began to row for the other side of the river to get his two guys fishing. There were wagers placed amongst the four clients as to who would catch the first fish, the most and get the best picture for each of the three days. But the ground rules were vague as to whether everyone had to begin fishing at the same time. So I got down to my boat to see them rowing for the other bank whilst talking smack about how they were going to win the first bet. Then I looked into my boat and saw somewhere in the neighborhood of four inches of standing water. The "butt" plug had popped out under the weight of the gear-laden transom and water had been gushing in for the last ten minutes. But before I began the long process of bailing *Ruby* out, I handed a conveniently rigged nymph rod to Jonathan -the guy who had booked and paid for the trip- and told him to cast five feet out, fifteen feet above the boat. On his first cast, he hooked, played and landed a fifteen-inch Redband. First bet down. Then I set about wearing myself weary bailing my boat out. By then I was both soaked with rain and clammy with sweat. We hadn't even pushed away from the ramp yet.

At our first stop, not far below the nasty little Trout Creek Rapid, we fished hard a spot known to hold some nice trout and got nothing. So we moseyed down to a spot I call "Righties". This run had been one of my more consistent dry fly zones on previous trips, so I sent Jonathan up towards the head riffle with the Chubby stick and got my other guy back in with the nymph rod. Only a couple minutes later I heard that particular, astonished angler's call of having a fish eat a great big, ridiculous Chubby. Jonathan had experienced his first. And he liked it. There wouldn't be a ton of Salmonfly action as the day went on. Instead, something else happened. The Green Drake came off. This is an even more rare treat down there, a mayfly in the size ten range that loves a crappy spring day. And this was it. After lunch, as we drifted into one long run with a treed-in bank on the right, there were fish just clobbering the bug. It was a completely different sight than we'd gotten used to during the Salmonfly bonanza. Then, it's the sporadic bankside explosion. This was constant activity. Every fish along that bank had changed focus and was now eating big mayflies in the most gluttonous fashion. We stopped and switched up to the biggest mayfly pattern I had. Jonathan was quickly into a proper slab, hooting as he shot the whole thing on his GoPro. There were so many fish up and so many bugs it was hard to know where to cast. A little farther downstream, in a long riffle leading into an even longer run, there were a hundred fish rising. The boys took turns picking a few off before we had to start rowing for camp. It was an experience I'd heard about but never seen and it made me wish for nasty weather a lot more often during the Salmonfly "hatch".

The other thing of note as May wears on and the fish eat as many of the big bug as they can fit in their bellies, is that with all the protein they take in, they get just obscenely powerful. The Redbands become steroid-addled versions of their already strong selves. So each battle is an extraordinary thing. If I had a fiver for every time I saw a slabby Redband jump one direction while the freshly tossed Chubby flew in the other, I'd be retired. It is something that happens as often as it doesn't. The fish just keeps launching, doing its best Tarpon imitation, until the Chubby comes loose. The barrel rolls and headshakes take on a new vigor as well, although because we're generally fishing with a heavy tippet there's a better than normal chance to hang on if the fish stays submerged. But it they take flight, especially repeatedly, the odds are stacked in their favor. And that's not just with clients. None of us are immune to that version of an ass kicking during Salmonfly.

Then there's the added bonus that for about a month every year we get to say "Chubby" a lot. Some are put off at first. They just can't shake the sexual connotation. Others embrace it right away and enjoy the simple pleasure of getting to talk about their Purple Chubby often and proudly. We grow accustomed to otherwise grown men whose lives require a certain decorum uttering phrases like, "You wouldn't believe the way my big purple Chubby got eaten today," or "That explosion on my gold-bodied Chubby was incredible," or, in the middle of a drift "Eat my Chubby, damn it!" Things like that. So we have a bit of fun for a while. It comes on abruptly and ends the same way. Just one day we stop spending our days thinking of new and unusual ways to talk about our Chubby.

Which brings me back to my wife's nipples. I've been home for a couple days, a half dozen time during each I swathe my disgusting paws with lotion. They're actually getting better. Michelie's upstairs working, I'm guessing right in between important tasks. I gotta go.

Chapter 9

Her Heart Goes All Aflutter

June

The fly, a client-tied CDC Caddis, alighted no more than a foot from limp grass at the river's edge. It was late-June on the Lower Deschutes River between Warm Springs and Trout Creek, the "Day Stretch". We were engulfed in near-suffocating heat. My drift boat, *Ruby Redside*, was under one of the only proper shade trees on the nearly ten-mile stretch of river, my other client sitting in one of the front seats. We had been grinding over this fish. From the rock I was perched on I knew my guy, Jonathan, a man I've known for three decades, had finally put the fly right where it needed to be. From thirty feet away we watched the fish -yes, that fish, the one we'd watched eat dozens of naturals as we worked on the perfect presentation- tip up and swirl the fly into the other side of its massive head. Standing high enough to see the whole thing, I gasped having realized how big this Redband was. In two rapid blinks of an eye it was bolting for the middle of the river. My friend, Steve, staying in a house nearby and having witnessed the entire scene, offered a fist bump as I jumped from my rock into the river downstream and got ready to coach Jonathan through playing the fish. Then everything changed.

Every now and again a guide such as myself has one of those weeks where the stars line up and I'm reminded why I love this job so much. To fully appreciate why this week was so revered by me, it's important to know that merely one week prior I was to be seen on the hot pavement in front of our fly shop in a fetal position, uttering profanities to disinterested ants as my back spasmed so intensely as to render my hard-earned ability to walk useless. The episode began innocuously enough that morning as I lifted a cooler into my truck to begin another day of guiding. *Just a tweak, no big deal.* Fast forward a couple hours to reaching abruptly forward so as to grab a twelve year-old year girl from face planting into the Crooked River, as she applied just a little too much energy into the very first cast of the day. A tear to one of the horizontal "balancing" muscles in my back occurred then. The girl was spared an early and inelegant end to her day. I continued to guide all four clients over the following four hours, barely disguising the increasing discomfort. My back has yet to fully recover. Between the river and our shop, I found myself unable to walk when I stopped to pick up some Valerian Root extract at a store on the east side of town. That was an especially disconcerting experience; literally being unable to put one foot in front of the other. I found myself leaning over the front of my scalding hot truck, trying to breathe through the pain, willing my body to move towards the store. Several people ate lunch at tables in the shade not twenty feet off the bow of the big truck. I did eventually shuffle to the front door. The first employee within earshot was asked the location of the Valerian Root. She busily replied, "Oh, that's right over here. Follow me." And with that she fled and disappeared. I hadn't a chance of keeping up. After finding another employee and requesting the same information, I was told where to look. In that aisle, I found the alcohol-laced root, but not the one I was looking for. I'm quite sure if this episode had been filmed for Candid Camera (and yes, I'll forgive you if you've never heard of the famous 60's TV show) the sequence would have appeared hilarious. From my perspective, it was anything but. Every abbreviated attempt at a step produced breath-stealing pain. Most of the time I was simply trying to stay upright, to not collapse into a temporary display of overpriced tortilla chips as might some terrifically intoxicated person. To accomplish the purchase and get back to the truck was a major achievement. I chugged a few droppers full of the root and prayed for some relief. If you've never heard of this herbal remedy, it is considered, among other things, to work as an anti-convulsant and pain reliever. It is also commonly used as a cure for insomnia, hence the lack of need for alcohol being added. I've sworn by it for twenty years, as this high-mileage shell I inhabit has grown ever more rickety and prone to random episodes of acute discomfort.

I then made my way back towards the shop, where I needed to drop off waders and boots from my trip. Once there, as I got out of my truck, I quite simply went down. It was, I'm sure you can imagine, not one of my prouder moments. But I'm glad to report that after nearly six hours of chiropractic care from some dear friends of mine here in Bend, and a therapeutic day of netting Scott's fish for him on Crane Prairie, I was able to go last Monday morning. The four trips that I missed can't be made up, but in that moment as I writhed in the parking lot out front of the shop I had fears of a far worse prognosis.

So it was with some extra excitement I met clients at the Madras Safeway for a full day on the Lower Deschutes. David and Jude, both visiting from SoCal, would be my little experiment as to whether the back would hold or not. This was a day spent with new love, a couple in their forties having just encountered one another six months ago. I was aware of that pure, dawning appreciation two humans have for each other in the "court and spark" phase. The adoration they shared was palpable for every moment of our day together. He caught many fish on a mixture of flies, mostly nymphs but the occasional dry grab was there to be had. She had never held a fly rod. As is often the case, the "blank canvas" angler took to the routine beautifully. She fooled many fish throughout our eight hours but perhaps, more importantly, the two of them bonded in a realm unfamiliar to both, soaking in the spectacle and grandeur of the Lower Deschutes. I felt the love from my rower's seat and especially enjoyed the quiet, wordless moments as they each absorbed the experience. I felt inspired and lucky to share their moment. It made me crave one with my wife, a breath in time to rekindle, reflect, share solitude and beauty, uninterrupted.

A couple days later, in the peak of this heat wave, I took two brothers visiting from California for a back-to-back with a camp out at Trout Creek. We had unreal fishing through the sweltering days. And when I say "sweltering" I refer to right around 110 degrees from mid-day till early evening. Both days. The canyon crackled under the oppressive sun. Even the usually maddening winds had abandoned the canyon.

We swam after every stop. But in these ridiculous conditions the caddis finally exploded, creating that "blizzard" hatch we've all heard about but seldom been there for. The fish weren't on them immediately, but by lunch there were big Redbands lurking in every eddy, big and small, splashing at the flittering bugs. At every stop there was a grab, or three. Some of these fish were middling, in the 12-14" range. Some not so.

Which brings me back to the beginning. The fish that ate Jonathan's fly -the CDC caddis his brother had tied- had been working the bank right in front of the anchored boat for twenty minutes. Sometimes it took a caddis, sometimes a PMD. But it just kept eating. We spent many, many minutes atop our respective rocks, strategizing, perfecting the cast, waiting out zephyrs, trying to time the fish's feeding pattern. We could tell it was a nice fish. But when it all came together, our collective breath was taken. After it rolled on Jonathan's fly and processed it's error in judgment, I watched it bolt by on its way to the depths of mid-river. Right away I recognized that this Redband was perhaps closer to two feet than 20". But after I'd jumped from the rock and stood waist-deep, just as the fish sailed three-feet clear of the river, that's when we all saw how thick it was. This was a one in a million down there, for sure one of the largest Redbands I've ever seen. I'd love to tell you about how the fish was played beautifully, netted skillfully, handled with great care, show you all the pictures of exhausted trout and trout bum. But the sad, and not even remotely surprising reality, is that this fish would not be landed. Nope, it would eventually make a run for the opposite bank at such a rate as to overwhelm the breaking strength of the tippet material. We all felt the taut line go slack. There was the moment each of us has endured, wherein nature's lack of sympathy or compassion lords heavily over us; when we feel as if somehow the universe conspired to elevate our spirit only to destroy it. This is a moment when Christians doubt the existence of God and Atheists question if perhaps they should have believed. There really are no words to comfort. Then Steve, the guy staying at the house down there chimed in, "Dude, that was awesome! That's easily the biggest trout I've ever seen on this river." It took Jonathan many minutes to shake the angst. I silently sympathized with him, just letting him feel whatever he needed to feel, but I knew there were no words to console.

I'm happy to report that later in the day Jonathan landed a ridiculously powerful fish after a masterfully fought battle. I will tell you that in the moment when the trout folded into net I felt the weight lift. The photo of us with the fish tells the story of a man worn out by heat, self-doubt, the realization that in this place neither he nor anybody else is completely in control, that we all take good with bad and somehow it all melds into an experience barely understood, so out of the norm as it is. The canyon and her river couldn't give less a shit about any of us. In a world wherein we coddle and protect ourselves and loved ones at every turn, being in such a treacherous, uncaring and harsh place requires of us to tap into a place in our spirit left unbothered normally.

For four of the next five days, as the extreme heat abated slightly, I guided brothers, a forty-something and his dad, a forty-something and his 20 year-old son, people from as far west as Hawaii, south as Los Angeles, east as Cleveland. We landed so many stunning rainbows, some beastly whitefish, a couple obscene "Butter Bellies" and one truly mesmerizing Bull Trout. To a man, there was an awe for the canyon and its inhabitants that revives me when tired, motivates me to greet each day, each trip, with renewed vigor and focus. Each trip *matters*. Nothing is taken for granted. I'm a lucky trout bum to be sure. And even now, as exposed flesh resonates heat and eyelids droop, I can't wait to get back down there.

Chapter 10

When the Passion Falls Limp

Mid-Summer

As a Lower Deschutes guide for a while now I've gotten accustomed to certain patterns throughout the season. You know, the frenetic scene that is the Opener; then the migration of big stoneflies; the event that is Salmonfly, with all the people, pinky-sized bugs crawling up your neck and colored up Redbands launching out of the river for the bounty; the brief doldrums before caddis, then blizzards of tentwings covering every surface of the boat; the heat of July during which you hope for a bikini hatch as much as any aquatic insect; the uncrowded "Dog Days" spent wet wading, searching for shaded eddy water and nymphing little bugs for big riffle fish; pre-steelhead September when we begin to fish some bigger flies just in the hopes....; the arrival of the first chromers and the insanity that prevails, all the way until the line freezes in your guides as you hope for one more grab before the season ends.

Now we are fully ensconced in the "Dog Days" a term referring to the hottest period of the year, reckoned in antiquity from the heliacal rising of Sirius, the Dog Star, in case you were wondering. Typically we have fifteen or sixteen hours of daylight and temps from ninety to ninety-five degrees. The canyon grass has long since browned over. All wildlife pretty much takes a siesta from eleven in the morning till six or so. The fish though, well, they keep eating. In the "Day Stretch" of the Lower D we are close enough to the dam that the water stays at around fifty-five degrees; hospitable for the trout and perfect for wet-wading all day long. As much as many local anglers and guides look for other places to fish during the "Dog Days", I like it down there, if for no other reason that they've gone elsewhere.

From *my* seat in the boat I've come to expect the fishing to be one way or the other on most days. Yea, it makes a difference if the anglers are really experienced and can present flies well right off the bat. But more often than not, the freshie angler learns the basic techniques quickly and begins hooking up. I have pre-planned stops based on who's in the boat. Days go by at a pace I dictate. Lunches are prepared in favorite shaded spots. Familiar rigs are applied. Fish are fooled. Clients are happy. It doesn't matter at all to them that I have the day mapped out from ramp to ramp. What I did the previous day or string of days isn't even on their radar.

I've actually come to love this time of the year. The predictability isn't boring; the challenges are still there, just different from other times of the season. As an angler who's been fortunate to fish a lot of day floats, I've come to the conclusion that the Lower Deschutes from Warm Springs to Trout Creek is easily my favorite, if for no other reason than it is constantly offering equations to solve. There is no standing in the front of the boat, drifting lazily along, casting hoppers at the bank. Everyday is a new set of pieces to a beautiful, kaleidoscopic and difficult puzzle. Yes, I am still fascinated and romanced. Completely. But even with all things intriguing, a little boredom can set in from time; comfortable familiarity swinging the door open for ennui.

All that changed a couple weeks ago when a fire began burning up the hill from the river just outside the town of Warm Springs. It is reported that some guy towing a fifth wheel got a flat, drove the rubber off the steel, began showering the roadside with sparks, eventually starting six small fires over a three mile stretch of road. I've heard that people were pulling along side him and alerting him to what was happening and he just kept driving. Good stuff. For several days the conflagration raged at will, everything in its path was endangered. Some areas were evacuated. Word came in that the fire had made it to the river but hadn't jumped from the west bank to the east. Bureau of Land Management let us know that the river was open but the conditions were dangerous to anyone with sensitive lungs or heart. We monitored the conditions day-to-day, knowing that we had a bunch of trips booked, beginning with a corporate outing on August 15th. That day, right up until the call came from the first of my guides down at the ramp, I wasn't sure if we had a river to fish for the fifteen guys showing up. The word finally came in that the river was open but really, really smoky. My instructions were to get everybody in boats and row downriver till the smoke eases. As it turned out, they all had a great time that day. The canyon was a little smoky but not dangerous. By mid float the smoke wasn't an issue at all. Sadly the fish were not willing to play very much. Turns out they are not cool with flames licking at their house.

It would be four more days till I was back down there with clients. Friday dawned clear and beautiful, a plume of smoke rising straight into the calm morning sky a little ways south and west of Warm Springs. I'd spend the day with a newlywed couple from California. I met Josh the previous season and he somehow talked his bride into a guided fly-fishing trip as part of their honeymoon adventure to Oregon. His new wife, Camilla was game for a trip down the big river, so off we went. Their initial motivation was lacking due a long night of sampling our local beers, but it didn't take long for the canyon to absorb us and enliven the senses, as is her wont. At our first stop they both hooked and played fish. The insects down there right now are small and represent a smattering of different bugs. The hot imitations have been little caddis and mayfly nymphs presented on light tippet. Good news is that with a proper presentation there's a solid chance of getting a trout to eat it. Bad news is that often times hanging on to the fish can be practically impossible. We even had a resident steelhead eat a small nymph at our first stop. It was an expectedly brief encounter, but exciting nonetheless.

Camilla found out several times just how unsocial our native trout, once hooked, can be. I felt for her as the day progressed and her frustration mounted. She stayed at it though, positive and focused, fooling quite a few fish before one came to the net. It was a fine bit of fishing by someone who'd never touched a fly rod prior to our day together.

There were startling reminders as we floated how much had burned right along the river's edge. Expanses of hillside, a week prior tan with waving grass, are now blackened, exposing a surprisingly rocky surface. The massive letters and shapes once discernable in the form of exposed rock amongst the native grass across from Mecca Flat are gone, as is the hundred foot-tall scorpion the next run down is named after. I wondered if they'll return with the grass, or perhaps new designs will emerge. Either way, it's a new landscape down there in the first few miles of the drift.

As the day wore on, more fish were fooled, we had a casual streamside lunch, fished some more. There was laughter from the front of the boat. The warm winds pushed up canyon, pulled back down, played havoc with casting one minute and rowing the next. At some point there was that deep sigh as we all realize how fortunate we are to be right there, just then. But I think what will stay with me from our day together is how lucky I was to spend it with people nearly half my age, embarking on a whole new, uncharted trip; excited, together, a new and formidable team. I'm quite sure a wonderful future awaits.

My clients the next day were a couple guys from Southern California in our area for a group cycling gathering. On their day off from riding they decided to check out our river. It was somewhere outside Redmond I noticed the smoke thickening. By Madras it was heavy, drooping into every tree branch, hovering atop the alfalfa fields. I would find out soon it was the Washington fires that created all the smoke, now being delivered via winds from the north. The smoke was following the Columbia south and then west, much of it eventually hanging a left up the Deschutes and then pushing ninety miles up to where we were planning on fishing. The smoke would make its way all the way to Bend by day's end. And as far west as Portland and the Willamette Valley, areas reported the worst air conditions on record. We pushed ahead to the ramp, determined to make a day of it in spite of the smoke.

The thick haze down in the canyon made for a spectacular sunrise. We rowed downriver to our first stop with a great orange ball leading the way. Right away we were into fish, landing some beautiful Redbands. Same flies and techniques from the last trip. Same stops. Different clients, wearing familiar smiles. We pulled over for a proper lunch that day, grilled steak, Caesar salad, chips and salsa. They each enjoyed a cold beer. All was right in the lives of these men, far from their normal trappings. They laughed, told stories and gave each other crap. It was men acting as boys, releasing tensions, allowing the canyon to be the only reality that mattered for those precious hours. As with the previous day, the little bug on fine tippet was key to fooling fish. The bigger stonefly imitation would still get the occasional trout or whitefish, but the #20 mayfly nymph far out produced everything else combined. I'd tell you what the fly was, but you know I need to think about job security! Who knows, maybe if you ask really nice...

After a day off during which I fished with my son, it was back to the "Day Stretch" for two more days. These trips were unique to this season in that each day I only had one person in the boat. Monday my client was the fabulous and famous Kim Reichhelm, she of multiple world championships in the realm of big mountain extreme skiing.

Kim is recovering from major back surgery in the spring that has curtailed the usual super-rad lifestyle of a woman who spends more time skiing, kite boarding, surfing, etc., than most of us can conceive. She now runs a ski tour business based out of Aspen but travels the world with clients in search of steep mountains and light powder. She is a massively talented athlete having achieved so much through incredible amounts of hard work, strong self-belief and almost inhuman bravado. Turns out Kim is a pretty skilled angler too. But more importantly, she possesses the critical trademark of all aspiring anglers: she's curious and can take stern instruction.

Kim picked up all the preciously important techniques needed on that stretch of river really quickly. The longer tension casts, sophisticated mends and feeding line into extended drifts were all needed to reach and fool some of the tougher fish in the river. And everywhere we stopped trout were caught. Her back held up well throughout the day, which was a pleasant surprise. We ate as I rowed from honey hole to honey hole. The smoke wafted up and down the canyon, sometimes borderline uncomfortable, sometimes nearly nonexistent. We ended up at Trout Creek where we'd camp. She wanted to see what our overnight program was like in hopes of both booking future multi-day trips and also promoting us within her client base. So I set her up with a cozy tent, we fished a little evening caddis, had a good meal and then I laid a cot out not thirty feet from the softly whispering river. The day was, by all accounts a guide's dream; skilled angler, interesting client, uncrowded fishing, lots of beautiful trout willing to play, a cot near the river and some good tequila. Yes, a lucky boy I am to have called that day "work".

Tuesday morning dawned relatively smoke free as we made coffee, broke camp and made for the Madras Safeway where Kim's car and my next client awaited. My guy for the day was David Morrow, a retired Air Force fighter pilot, a three decade veteran who rose to the rank of Admiral while moving his family over a dozen times during his career. David is a good guy with a healthy interest in angling. He's decided to call Oregon home for he and his wife in their retirement years and wants to get proficient at a few different techniques for fooling fish on a fly rod.

The only wrinkle in the plan was that David is fundamentally deaf, by which I mean he ALWAYS wears a hearing aid, except for our day because he was worried about it getting wet. Typically, this wouldn't have been a huge issue. But these days on the Lower D we've had a big algae bloom. And since we're nymphing most of the time, it's not uncommon to pick up junk on the bugs. Part of my job is cleaning bugs. Instead of just dropping the flies back in the river before the next cast, I hold them and when I say "go" the client cast and I let go simultaneously. This works great when the client can hear. Not so great with David. Not once, not twice, but three times during our day he went to cast before the "magic word". The last time I was holding a #10 Jimmy Legs. The point of the hook buried straight to the bone. I'm sure I squealed like a gutted pig but he didn't hear it. The hook was de-barbed so it came out easily enough. But my finger has this amazing bruise. And it still hurts like hell. The other two times was just little nymphs, paled in comparison. Me being the deeply philosophical man you all now know me to be, I chalked the day up to karma, the great and gorgeous goddess of fate, seeing to it that I know how it feels for the fish.

We fooled many trout throughout the day, mostly on the same doomed rig of a tiny nymph on fine tippet in relatively heavy water. He had a great attitude, understanding that simply getting the fish to eat your offering out there nowadays is a victory. Playing and landing big trout on gear that light is the bonus. He even hooked a nice fish on the switch rod at one stop, swinging a Sculpzilla in the right spot, the right way. I was impressed with how hard he was willing to work on new techniques, how accepting he was of new perspectives. We enjoyed our day together immensely.

I drove back down 97 last night through the smoky gloom, reminiscing over some incredible days down there. The Lower Deschutes from Warm Springs to Trout Creek has become my office more than any other river. Without going back through my journals I believe those last two were days fifty-one and fifty-two working down there this season. Yet somehow when I'm away from her for a few days, I miss every aspect of her. I simply can't get enough.

Chapter 11

Our Pulse Quickens

August

As an introduction to this story, firstly I must offer apologies for its length. No fishing story should be this long. But I had a day off from the river and felt like writing. So grab a fresh cup of coffee, or a beer depending on the time of day. Secondly, please read with tongue firmly lodged in cheek as that is how it was written; this is meant to be kinda fun...

For those of us who fish through the seasons here in Central Oregon few things give the sense of summer waning into fall as much as the first sighting of a migrating steelhead in the upper stretch of the Lower Deschutes. Note how I clarified a "migrating" steelhead. That is because, believe it or not, there are steelhead that call the Deschutes "home". These are fish that were either bound for another Columbia River tributary and got distracted, only to decide that our beloved "big river" seemed a good place to stay, or a genuine Deschutes fish that simply resisted nature's beckoning back to the salt after spawning. I know, the biologists are all frothing at the mouth in disagreement right now. All two of you. But please, sit back down and hear me out. I, along with many other guides, spend a lot of time on that river. You know, *a lot*. Some of us to the point that this time of year it's the days not down there that disorientate, make us wonder what to do with ourselves without worrying over the next oar stroke, the next riffle, run, pocket or bank to probe, where to prepare lunch, the dreaded thought of whether or not there's a cold beer in the cooler to help stow the boat at the take-out ramp. You know, the important things that our worlds revolve around. This is our daily routine; it is where patterns make sense, where we feel purpose and meaning. Yea, we are on the river a lot. So to both you biologists out there, just let me go on. Put your computer back down. No need to hurl it across the room, not just yet.

As I was saying, there are steelhead in the Lower Deschutes year-round. Why do I state this so unequivocally? Well, because I've seen them. Not just once or twice. Not all the time either. But enough to know. The scenario is usually pretty much the same. Some unwitting client fishing a 5wt trout rod with two, maybe three bugs under a bobber, making adequate drifts through some random seam (this is where I perhaps stray from detailed, specific locations, as there are a couple spots that lack "random-ness"), and when said bobber goes down and I have to distract them from whatever reverie they happen to be spacing out on to set the hook, our collective world erupts as a five-pound steelhead surges at the end of their line. There's a saying we perhaps overuse in this business: "Seen *that* movie before." It's usually in reference to something not great happening, repeatedly. Like a guy trying to wade too far out into "Little Indian" riffle, slips and goes headlong into the current. Or an angler continuously casting over their right shoulder from a river left station, even though the wind is howling downstream, eventually impaling himself. These are occurrences wherein we might utter the time-honored phrase, "Oh yea, seen that movie before". You know, because we know how it ends... You get it, right? Okay, apologize for talking down. But you are all anglers, so I can take nothing for granted.

Where was I? Oh yea, perhaps a dozen times a season at some "random" spot a client will hook a steelhead on say the 5th of June, by which time we are down to 4 or 5X tippet, even 6 ocassionally, and some #16 & 18 flies. Can you guess how this particular movie ends? The truth is there are a few different endings, none of which has the fish folded, over-stuffing a trout net. Nope, that's just not how it ends. As much as we'd love to see the Hollywood hero and heroine embracing now and forever back dropped by some tropical sunset, sheathed in white linen; a magnificent, tear-inducing, symphonic crescendo filling every emotional sense you possess. Nope. This is the one where the plane doesn't land safely; the firefighters arrive moments too late; the passenger train bound for wherever departs the depot, leaving a forlorn lover standing alone, destined to forever be. Remember the James Bond movie where he gets married, is off in some rad Aston Martin with his new, smokin' hot bride and same baddies riddle her with bullets intended for him? A cop pulls up and Bond tells him the girl is just napping, that they have all the time in the world to share. Really, one of the most gut-wrenching movie moments ever. Yea, it's like that. Only *harder* to watch.

Okay, so I feel I've digressed a little here. Already. Humble apologies.

This time of the year, while rowing certain stretches of the river, we stand with oars in hand over every tail out, every likely spot a steelhead might post up. We imagine great, broad-shouldered anadromous beasts spooking out from under our boat. Or maybe we didn't imagine it. Maybe that really was the first of the fresh fish, right where he ought to be. I had that moment a couple weeks ago just above the ramp at Trout Creek. Absolutely, positively a migrating fish, tucked in right where I see one every year, right where he rests up before pushing around the corner into heavy current. It's easy to understand why he's always there; a respite before the next effort. That night he'd push through the steep, shallow riffle the half-mile up to the next easing of velocity. Then he'd keep going, perhaps all the way to the dam. Anyway, I knew some steelhead were already in there but to see one with my own eyes gave a renewed sense of the time being nigh, the season being upon us.

Last week I hosted the Remedi brothers both born in the Midwest, both now relocated to the West. They've fished many rivers for many trout. They take such a trip every year. It was a pleasure to have them in my boat. We fooled a bunch of trout, including a lovely little Bull. Sadly, as is the case so often this time of the season when we are down to the aforementioned rigs, many fish broke off or shook free before succumbing to the net. But the day went well. Every stop produced some hook-ups. I was feeling really good, both for them and for me. It's always nice to stop for lunch and know that if another fish isn't caught, the day will still be considered a success. Lunch was grilled steaks, Caesar salad, some local chips and salsa. They enjoyed beer. Then after the cookies it was time to get them back in the river while I cleaned and packed. I sent them down to a little spot where I figured they could be trusted to fish without any real harm coming their way. Perhaps fifteen minutes later, just as I was finishing the packing or the boat, there was a great, panicked, almost guttural scream from down river. "GRIIIFFFF!" That was it. And it sounded bad. In the proverbial heartbeat I was heading their direction, having the presence of mind to snatch my pack. I'm guessing if there were a film crew present and rolling I'd have done a pretty good David Hasselhoff imitation. You know the way he grabs that little buoy thing on his way into the surf? That was me, only with my Fishpond Waterdance Guide pack and Nomad Series hand net cleverly attached, fearlessly venturing to where the distress signal had emitted. Vainglorious, I know, but I'm quite sure that is how it would have appeared on film. Quite sure indeed. Hmmmmm, just a moment to reflect on how awesome that would have looked... Where was I?

Oh yea, so down bank I ran, feeling pretty assured that I would find one of the brothers in some state of drowning. The call had been that of life-threatening panic. Someone had fallen in and was most likely clinging to an overhanging tree branch, moments from an inelegant death, the river bottom only inches beneath his studded boot soles. *So this is the day it happens*, I reflected inwardly.

Upon arriving on the bank above them I was more than a little surprised to find both brothers standing upright in the river, neither reckoning with death in any way. One was just upstream with a bent rod held high overhead. The other was perhaps forty feet downstream, peering into the river with a small trout net in hand. That would be Steve, an airplane mechanic from Arizona. The one with the bent rod was Kevin, a fireman living in Las Vegas. He looked up and asked, "You got your camera?"

"Yea, my phone's right here," I replied setting it up to snap some pictures.

"Awesome!" Kevin said, with a genuine enthusiasm. "I got something HUGE on here."

I looked up at Kevin, then down at Steve, examining the bend of the rod, the angle and tautness of the line, and then tried to gain some focus on what he had hooked down there. The general lack of commotion where the fish was laying lead me to believe that perhaps he'd got one of those big 'Butter Bellies", maybe even hooked somewhere other than the mouth... I reflected briefly that he was using a relatively light trout rod on very light tippet (but more on that later) and seeing as though the river quickened just downstream from him, I'd just stay up there on the bank until it broke everything off. Not trying to be a negative Nellie or anything. Just then Steve made an abrupt stab into the river with the little teardrop net.

And the movie began.

As it was, the net actually jabbed the fish. And the fish turned out to be a steelhead. And it didn't like being jabbed. It blew up right in front of Steve, no more than fifteen feet off the bank. "Steve," I said utilizing my least flippant tone. "Get out of the water. Grab my phone and stay on the bank." Then in Kevin's direction, "Hey Kevin, you got a steelhead on here. So let's just try to keep some even pressure and see what he does." As I slid into the river with the relatively new Fishpond Nomad Series carbon fiber trout net at the ready, I tried to keep an eye trained on the fish. It was a solid one; four to five pounds, and just dogging in the drop-off water twenty feet out. In assessing the situation, I came up with the following: 1) His knots were sound because we'd re-rigged right after lunch. 2) Above the split shot was 4x, below it went 5x to the first fly and 6x to the others. 3) The largest fly was a size eighteen Anato-May with a similarly sized Trina's Angelcase BWO emerger and number twenty Olive Soft Hackle behind it. 4) We were pretty much screwed. I positioned myself thirty or forty feet below Kevin. From there I kept an eye on him, anticipating that I'd have some sagacious advice to bestow. Yet minute after long minute he had the rod in the perfect position, bent nicely into the fish that for the time being, it appeared, had forgotten was hooked. Now this wasn't just any rod, mind you. No, we're talking about an Echo rod. And not just any Echo rod, but the Echo Carbon series in a nine-foot 5wt. The rod was equipped with the glorious little Echo ION 4/5 reel. Both have been in the boat for three long seasons, enduring abject abuse at the hands of countless clients. I actually have two such set-ups, monikered Echo 5wt Number One and Echo 5wt Number Two. They are, without doubt or suspicion, rods worthy of such esteemed appellations. Not sure which one Kevin was now bending so epically into the steelhead, but I knew in his capable hands that the Umpqua Feather Merchants fluorocarbon tippet would be protected as would his first-born. It was a moment of symmetry; water, sun, sky, ghosts of ancient tribes, otter, osprey, all that's ever been or will ever be, present, witnessing the struggle. You could almost feel the stars align. A man waist deep in the mighty

Deschutes River confronting an ornery denizen. A tug of war proposing historic proportions. And yet it would only ever end one way. The movie was surely nearing that moment you can barely stand to watch. My certainty of the outcome was unwavering. And yet the tippet held.

The fish made a dash for the middle of the river. The tippet held. The fish somersaulted repeatedly. The tippet held. The fish got downriver and rubbed the line on a rock. The tippet held. Who had tied these knots of steel you might ask. Well, that'd be me. Suddenly the sun shone brighter. God? Is that you? No, just the day wearing on into the afternoon. Or maybe it was. Who am I to say? I'm just a guide who ties superlative knots. But enough about me. Kevin was really the man of the hour. Somehow he maintained perfect pressure on the fish, able to steer him away from the rock the steelhead and I were behind. Several times I thought to attempt a net job, but discretion got the better part of valor. And throughout all of this, the tippet held. I've seen a lot of duress inflicted on light tippet before, but never anything like this. Boy, that Umpqua fluorocarbon is the real deal. I'll tell ya that much. And the Echo Carbon nine-foot 5wt must be the most capable big fish-fighting rod ever constructed from anything other than bamboo. But I digress yet again.

For some reason, perhaps ten minutes into the fight, the steelhead simply cruised back above the rocks we'd been behind for so long. I climbed back level with the fish and began girding myself for the decisive moment wherein I'd masterfully scoop the beast into the net. Most of us guides have been in this situation: we want to get it over with so badly that we start strategizing how to get the fish landed, sometimes perhaps prematurely, sometimes perhaps even losing the fish in the process. Having broke off a client's steelhead last season only to feel his wrath for the rest of the day, I've gotten a little more circumspect about just thrusting my net at a fish. But, with this one, I knew we had to get it done. You can only hold your breath for so long. All the steelhead was doing now was going out ten or fifteen feet, giving a few headshakes and then finning back no more than five feet from me. This happened several times and on each I imagined getting the net under it. On perhaps the fifth or sixth move, I went for it, punching the gorgeous, lightweight net in and down and then forward. I won't claim to be the most stylish netter of fish. No, that distinction would irrevocably belong to my co-worker, Dave. But in this case the frantic scoop resulted in the great fish folding heavily into the new net, which had just earned its exorbitant price tag.

What followed immediately were the obligatory high-fives, deep, relaxed breaths, a war hoot echoing off canyon walls. And me, standing over the fish, stunned. This steelhead had eaten the Trina's. And so, yes, here was incontrovertible evidence that steelhead eat insects when back in the fresh. Sorry you two biologists. That's just how it is. Deal with it. You've permission to heave your computer against the nearest wall now. The tiny fly was lodged fairly in the corner of the mouth. But the other flies and tippet were wrapped around the head to the point where only six inches of tippet remained below the split shot. Still, that means the fish was landed on 5x.

Shortly thereafter I realized it was a hatchery fish. When I announced to the guys that we'd have to kill it they were a little bummed. But as I looked for the right rock, I explained why such fish are in the river and the importance of dispatching of them when they are caught. Those who know me understand that this is difficult to do. Hatchery fish or no, this one has lived a hardcore life, enduring life-threatening hardship we can't even begin to comprehend, unless you've done battle in a godless war. The hatchery fish, pale as they may be in comparison to their wild relatives, had to run the same gauntlet to get to the sea as a mysterious and no doubt highly annoying homing beacon beeped incessantly; the same rigorous tenure in the salt, chasing baitfish while being chased by sea lion and orca; made the same insanely arduous journey back up the Columbia, the beacon even louder now, climbing ridiculous fish ladders, skirting nets, remarkably avoiding perverted amounts of human-induced torment; eventually hanging a right turn -for reasons they can't begin to comprehend- into the Deschutes; somehow avoiding a thousand seductively swung flies by the time they pass Maupin; and then pushing up another thirty miles of river; all the while watching countless hundreds of brethren succumb to one hazard or another; only to make the innocuous mistake of nibbling a tiny mayfly imitation offered by a guy from Vegas still burping up his steak lunch and cold beer. Perhaps I romanticize this simple act of nature. But every time I cradle a steelhead, my heart overflows with astonishment and adoration. To take its life is just never easy. I know why these hatchery fish are in the river and have grown accustomed to what needs to befall them, but I still give a little prayer each time. I call it "Eddy's Prayer" in honor of the love interest in the book "The River Why", a brilliant tome by the then quite young David James Duncan. In the book our love struck protagonist Gus watches Eddy capture a crawdad and before twisting its tail off to use for bait, she whispers to it, "Life's short. It's God's fault. I'm sorry" And so that is what I said to this steelhead just before the first of the five or six blows it took to finally render it inanimate, releasing, at last, the proud fish into the waters of another, better world; a cleaner, undammed river.

Steve went in to make a few casts as Kevin and I walked up to the boat where he posed for a few pictures with the beautiful, lifeless fish. We talked reverently of its journey and how lucky we were to have encountered it, and what a fine bit of angling it took to land such a fish on the tackle we had. Then I broke my rule of not drinking on the job with a few sips of a beer. That was my first steelhead of the year and was worthy of some ceremony. Most of the beer went into the river as part of my prayer and thanks, an invocation that the river and I might be able to continue this mind-blowing relationship we've forged over these last four years. The beer was offered as a humble request that this be the first of many such fish we encounter over the next few months.

After the inglorious placing of the fish in the cooler, Kevin went to get his brother. I sat on Ruby's gunnel and exhaled deeply. The emotions were that of confused reflection. The movie hadn't ended at all the way I expected. Like all the greatest films, this one had the twist, the mis-direction leading you down one path only to divert you unwittingly to another; so masterfully done as to cause a brief lack of balance. Perhaps a European directed this particular movie. You know what I mean? Ever seen those movies that end and you're thinking, "No way! That's the stupidest thing I've ever seen." I know, me too. Pisses me off.

Only I actually like this one.

So I sat there in the emptying theater, shedding a confused tear, eating the last of my soggy, cold popcorn, cogitating. It would still be days before it made sense. Or maybe I just imagined it made sense because I need answers, clarity, closure. Maybe sometimes we need things to not make sense so the rest of our lives seem reasonable. Or maybe sometimes we are presented a certain cache of elements, external and otherwise, meant to propagate a deeper, almost painfully philosophical internal dialogue; the most often difficult and uncomfortable straddling of a fence between what we can and what we can't explain. Maybe events occur only to disorientate; to disembowel everything we *think* we know. Or maybe I should shut the hell up and go catch another fish.

Against a spine of volcanoes
Reaching into the heavens
Near the bottom of the earth
She leans
I'll dream of her every contour

Chapter 12

When Her Servant Rebels

Recently, I hosted two clients on the Lower Deschutes River from Warm Springs to Trout Creek for a day of fly fishing. Now, before I continue it should be noted that almost any day of the week since late April I could have begun a story with that exact same line. It's getting old, I know. But bear with me on this one, because it ends a little differently than most. My clients: Ed, a homebuilder here in Bend, and Dan, a guy Ed built a home for. Dan was a quarterback for OSU back in the "Giant Killer" era. Pretty rad. We met before daybreak at the shop and carpooled up to the river. So instead of cranking NPR and chain smoking, I had company for the drive. They turned out to be interesting, cool and engaged. Both had some experience, but were eager to learn the subtle tactics used on the Lower Deschutes. We would be on the water by seven-thirty. The day was dawning clear, promising lovely weather.

September had proven to be one of my busiest months of the season. And while there have been steelhead in the system, the trout fishing has been so insanely good that most of the time we put on my tried and true nymph rigs and just catch fish. For those of you who have suffered through my recent stories, you know that steelhead have been known to eat said nymph rigs. So without belaboring the point, I haven't seen much need to specifically target steelhead. But anyway, yea, I've been down there a bunch recently and felt pretty confident in my flies as well as how and where to use them. The only downside to this mindset is that I've been using very light tippet to create these effective rigs. As told in earlier stories, these rigs fool fish, but can be problematic when it comes to landing the above-average trout. So several times on the drive up to the river several I tried to impress upon the guys how important it will be to really *play* the fish; to not horse a trout to the net, *dance* with it. I expressed that there is no magic bullet, no surefire tactic. I told them that if every fish danced the same way, my job would be easier; they'd land more and larger fish and I'd write a book explaining how to dance with large trout on light tippet called "How To Dance with Large Trout on Light Tippet", which would become an overnight sensation, hence propelling me into the highest echelon of fly-fishing notoriety; I'd be made fabulously wealthy; welcomed into the literary and social circles inhabited by Lani, Gierach, Lyons, Travers and Duncan; surrounded by feinting and fawning nubile lovelies all waving fly rods seductively, each more desperate than the others to earn my praise and undivided attention; I'd live in a massive house in Tetherow vaguely shaped like a trout, ensconced in a Triploid-filled moat; drive a customized Mercedes Sprinter van decked out with a see-through waterbed filled with Crooked River trout; my friends and family would speak gushingly at every opportunity about me and my mastery of all things Redband, constantly expressing reverie and wonder at what a remarkable fortune fly fishing had bestowed upon me. Yes, I told my already exhausted clients, if the fish all behaved similarly, things would be far different. But alas, the trout wish to play no part in my delusional fantasy world; they'd rather screw up every damned day for the last month and a half with their unsocial, camera shy idiosyncrasies. For, as many of you know from my previous, long-winded, insomnia-curing stories of late, the Lower Deschutes trout have proven a noble adversary when it comes to dancing them into the net. At some point in my forty-five minute soliloquy, I did feel Ed and Dan's collective attention drawn out of my truck cabin and into the pastel sky, no doubt wishing they'd driven themselves.

At our first stop of the day we were broken off six times. Occasionally we'd lose only one fly. Sometimes all three, and the split shot. I told them repeatedly it wasn't their fault, and some of the time it really wasn't. I reminded them that they were making the drift and fooling fish and isn't that cool enough? Yea, no. They wanted fish in the net. So did I. Ed had a bit more of a knack for playing them. We eventually landed a few really pretty trout, including a beautiful baby bull. After an hour or so, while upriver re-rigging Dan who'd been broken off again, Ed yelled that he had a fish on. I made my way down there wordlessly. He was getting with the program now, using the rod, feeling what the fish was doing and about to do instinctively. As a guide, one of the most rewarding moments is when I get to watch somebody learn the dance. They lead as much as follow. Reactions look planned. Nothing surprises. Ed and this fish were dancing. It was only thirty feet out, dogging hard in maybe six feet of water. The nine-foot, 5wt Echo Carbon was bending beautifully cork to tip. When I got alongside Ed, I noticed the line began moving upstream. This is something only the cockiest fish do. Lesser beings spastically thrash, desperate to relieve the pain and pressure. The big, old, nasty ones, well they're just pissed. You can almost hear them down there saying, "Aw crap, this again. Damn it! I'm such an idiot!

But seriously, who fishes stuff that small this time of the year?" Well, that'd be my clients and me. We do. So suck it, fish.

As I was saying, this one was down there mumbling to itself, swimming up river, just girding for the decisive bolt to deeper water, during which the line would break or the hook would dislodge. That's what he's done a hundred times. This season. I casually warned Ed that the fish would make a move before too long. It's a scenario I've witnessed enough times to know. Sure enough, in the proverbial blink of an eye, the fish turned for the middle of the river and took off with stunning alacrity. Ed reacted perfectly, dipping the rod just enough to let the reel start giving line. The Echo ION 4/5 reel whirred and buzzed for five solid seconds. Then the fish headed for the Columbia. Another fifty or sixty feet of line and backing disappeared. "We're taking a walk," I announced, grabbing the back of his waders, letting him know this was not up for discussion. Around a small bend and then down along the grassy bank, in two to three feet of water, we trekked in pursuit. Perhaps a hundred feet into the walk, Ed dancing with the fish beautifully just to my left, I positively clouted a submerged obstacle and was posthaste swimming along side him. There is large piece of garbage that's been in the river as long as I've been around. I've waded around it dozens of times. But on this day, with everything else in play, I simply forgot it was there. It's been a long time since I had the sensation of swimming in my waders. In this spot there's just nothing to push up on. The water is too deep. There are no rocks around. The current is strong enough to make it hard to get your feet back under you. It's just a really crappy place to fall in. Compounded by how quickly we were moving when I hit it, I bet I was face down for three or four seconds. Long enough, I'm quite sure, for cartoon bubbles to hatch from the surface, popping into "HELP!" and "IT'S REALLY COLD". If Dave were there he would have asked if I saw any fish while swimming. If any of you happened to be strolling up that bank just then, you'd have no doubt gotten a great guffaw out of it. As it was, only Ed was there to witness, and it turned out his attention was so focused out in the middle of the river, he actually missed most of the action behind him. Once right side up, having made a quick evaluation of all that had fallen out of my pack, and busily wringing out the sleeves of my Simms Fall Run jacket, assessing how much water had snuck between my substantial belly and the wading belt, I checked on Ed. He was doing great! From that moment I realized that he needed little coaching from me. We buddy waded through a couple sketchy spots and had to carefully navigate some overhanging branches. But for the most part he was doing everything as it should be done. Every time the fish got too close to shore it would bolt back out, tearing line from the reel. In that spot the fish had the better hand; we were doing everything right and yet this fish would not be landed until the topography dictated. We had covered at least a quarter-mile when we came to another overhanging tree. When we were fifty or so feet above it, a voice boomed, "Hey!! Where do you guys think you're going?" If I hadn't been completely sober I might have thought the tree was getting all *Wizard Of Oz* on us.

To some unseen entity I replied, "Oh, hey, sorry 'bout that. We got something big on here. Not entirely in control just yet..."

"Well, I'll be damned," the tree said. "Let me have a look." Then the tree barked.

The fish was now finning, almost calmly right in front of the tree. I told Ed to stay right where he was while I readied the trusty Fishpond Nomad Series net. Our best hope right then was that the fish didn't make another run. I figured it had to be pooped. Hard to say how much time had passed, but we'd been at it for a while. The tree guy was now standing just above us on the bank with his tree dog still barking that weak, *crap-they're-not-scared-of-me* bark.

This is rarely the most elegant part of the dance. Both fish and fisherman are exhausted. More flailing now than anything else. But still Ed needed almost no coaching. He felt that we were in the right spot. He sensed the fish beginning to succumb. I eased out just a little closer to the deep water. "Let's get 'er done, buddy," was the last bit of advice. Ed lifted the rod up a bit and as soon as the fish's head was above the surface, he led it to me. The fish, now and for the first time fully in view, surrendered, folding into the net. Ed rushed down to see. I was quietly, reverently praising this one. "Sorry, man. Sorry for the hassle. But you'll be alright." It was not, as I'd been imagining, a steelhead. It was far rarer, far more elusive, and far more badass. In the net was a five-pound butter belly sucker!!!

Just kidding.

It was a Redband rainbow trout. And without a tape we'll never know exactly how big, but I'll go on record claiming it right around 20". Now for those of you who spend your time ruthlessly hammering Wickiup "River" this time of the year, or lolling around Crane Prairie in fancy lake boats wearing flip flops, this may not impress. But for those of us who spend 120 days a year busting sac on the "Day Stretch" of the Lower Deschutes this was a fish to relish, to honor and give thanks for. And that is what we did. Then there was the obligatory photo. We put the fish back in the net and I spent a minute simply admiring every aspect of it. Big, muscular shoulders; perfect, torpedo-shaped body; radiant, silver-blue gill plate; powerful, red fins purpose-built for a big river; a flawlessly evolved creation if ever there was one. Sometimes I'm baffled by the way a trout can stir my entire being like that. Thirty years I've been wandering around with a fly rod. I'm crappy at math and have rarely chronicled exact numbers of fish caught, but I'd have to guesstimate, oh, I don't know, a couple thousand trout have graced my life. And this one, this great old Redband brought me to the verge of tears it was so beautiful. So I just cradled it for what seemed like a long time. Interestingly, even when the trout was strong enough to go, it stayed, almost as if appreciating my caress and admiration. Eventually, though, it gave a big kick and swam free into a new area of the river.

Ed and I crawled onto the bank and made our way towards where the odyssey had begun, me wringing out my jacket all the while. I tried calling the shuttle driver in hope that he hadn't left to get my rig and I could hike back for dry clothes. The day wasn't frigid, but it wasn't warm either. Not even a little. There was no answer. I'd spend the rest of the day with wet socks. No big deal. And anyway, there's no way I was going to rain on Ed's parade. The dude was stoked. We talked excitedly about the battle, the amazing trek down river, the brutish power of the fish. It was the biggest fish he'd ever caught on a fly rod. It was one of the biggest trout I've personally held on the Deschutes. It was a career moment for both of us, and a masterful dance on Ed's part. We popped over to the riverbank near the obstacle and found a couple things that had fallen out. There was still the matter of all the water in the pack's pockets and some wet fly boxes. I know, I know, I should zip everything up all the time. It's just that I, you know, NEVER fall in.

We eventually got back up to Dan, sorted his rig and then he farmed or broke off a few more fish. Then we moved on.

Not much more to report from the day until our last stop. Dan had yet to land a good trout so I put him on one of my honey holes and we began working it. He hooked up several times but either came undone or was broken off; still not *dancing*. There was a particular seam just below and a touch inside of where he was drifting that looked really fishy. So we set about working on the cast, the mend, the feeding of line, the next mend, so on and so forth. There was one little bit of the drift we just weren't getting so I offered to show him, just once, so he could get a visual. Can you guess what's about to happen? I know, it's painful for me too. Right when the bobber got to the spot, I made the last little mend, all the while explaining that right there is where I expect the fish to...BOBBER DOWN!

Bad Guide.

I set the hook and the area around the flies erupted in that sensory-bombarding explosion of movement and color; frantic, chaotic splashing, a thumping, other-worldly energy. Immediately I knew it was not a trout. Nope, this one was a steelhead. I got the impression that the hook set was solid, 9' 6-weight Winston LT bent perfectly with added pressure just to be sure the hook fully dug in. Beneath the bobber were a couple (maybe more!) split shot, a size sixteen something-or-other (not trying to be vague, it just doesn't really matter) on 5X, a size eighteen BWO Trina's Angelcase Emerger (that specific enough for ya?) on 6X and a number twenty Olive Soft Hackle also on 6X. So no matter how you slice it, this was a fish that most likely would not be landed. I asked Dan if he'd like to play it for, you know, four or five seconds. Even brief dances can be fun and exciting. He reached for the rod. I reluctantly handed it his way. Then he clutched the cork with both hands, gripping the line between palm and cork. Instinctively, and maybe because I'm a big fat jerk, I grabbed it back as quickly as it had been offered. And just then, the fish made for the other side of the river. With rod bowed and Battenkill reel shrieking I turned to Dan and explained that the line really just needs to be able to go out, you know, really quickly. Over by the far bank the fish rolled a couple times. I again offered the rod to Dan. This time, and maybe because I'm a big, fat jerk, he refused, saying he'd rather watch me play the fish; that he'd learn something. Cool. I'd get to play a steelhead on my soft old 6wt. Yea, this would be totally educational. All kinds of learning. So much learning it'll be like learning *from* learning.

The fish made a crazy move back to our side of the river, angling slightly down, throbbing, heaving, angry. This was the most uncommon gambol; not your wedding reception first dance. This was frenetic, mosh pit, crowd surfing lunacy. No familiar tryst, I don't care who you are.

Ed had begun wading in our direction, wondering aloud what all the commotion was about. I announced that we'd be taking a little walk and would he mind terribly grabbing the steelhead net from the boat. I know, I should have offered him the rod, huh? I'm such a jerk. Instead I started bossing my client around.

Bad guide.

As soon as the fish felt the shallow water on our side of the river it was on another reel-melting run to the far bank. "Come on, boys. We're heading downriver." Off we went, one client watching me play a fish on *his* rod, the other dutifully hauling the heavy wooden net, me with a steelhead thrashing eighty feet away; dancing.

Really bad guide.

At some point I quieted my guilty conscience enough to focus on actually landing the fish. Not sure exactly when I felt the tide turn, but for sure there was a moment when it occurred to me that I might actually be leading the dance. We were in a great spot where the bottom sloped quickly from the bank to deep water. The fish was no longer spastic. We wore it out there for another minute or two. Then I asked Ed to get downstream and be ready. We'd only get one good chance with the net. Once he was positioned I raised the rod tip up high and got the fish's head up just long enough to slide the entire thing into the net. There followed the quick congratulations and awkward high-fives. I put the rod on the bank behind us. Then we realized it was a hatchery fish. I explained to the boys that we'd have to dispatch this fish to other rivers; it could not be allowed to survive. We found a little spot on the bank with some properly-sized stones; I picked one the size of a grapefruit and then held the fish still. I stroked its firm shoulders, admiring every inch of its solid, powerful body. As explained in previous stories to previous clients, this fish had endured the same voyage, the same hardships as its wild relatives. And as much as we all know what must befall them, I still feel every anadromous fish deserves some dignity in their passing. And so some was given this fish. Then I saved it from any further torment on this earth.

We made our way back to the boat and readied the fish for the cooler. Ed was stoked to have a fish to take home to his son. They would clean it and put it in their new smoker. Before placing the fish in a bag, I asked if Ed wouldn't mind taking a picture of me with it. And like an obedient client, that is exactly what he did.

Bad Guide.

The rest of the afternoon passed without event, save for Dan finally landing a nice 'bow where we'd hooked the steelie. We enjoyed cold beers at the ramp while I stowed Ruby for the drive home. This was my last guide trip before heading to California for a few days so I took a little extra time getting the boat and my gear properly put away.

We made our way back to Bend as the sun rested atop the lower row of craggy teeth we call the Three Sisters, Broken Top and Bachelor. The boys had stories for their families. They were both psyched on their day spent in the canyon of the Lower Deschutes. I sat mostly in quiet shame.

The next morning, before leaving for California, I posted a picture on Facebook. It was of me smirking, and a two-foot long hatchery steelhead, not smirking. The afternoon sun looks as luxurious as it felt. The caption was something like: "This happened today on a demo cast for a client. Ate a #20 Olive Soft Hackle on 6X". By the time I got to Cali there was a hilarious series of comments, of which I'll share a few. Some were complimentary:

"Awesome, Griff"

"Wow"

"Gorgeous"

"I want one!!!"

Some were slightly snarkier:

"Sometimes you really piss me off!"

"Demo cast my ass! Must be a hatchery fish"

"The irony of this photo is that he had the CLIENT take the glory pic!!"

And then the Spey-centric crowd had to chime in.

"A swung fly is still a swung fly"

"Not if it's under bobber with three split shot"

"Real men swing flies under a bobber"

"Is that why he hides the rod for the photo?"

But there, amongst all the clatter, was my son, my favorite human and far and away my finest contribution, the increasingly fishy Jasper Marshall with a fittingly brief, poetic and concise comment.

It read simply, "Bad Guide"

Chapter 14

Her Most Beautiful Dark Side

Many of you have probably heard of Whitehorse Rapids, the defining stretch of the Lower Deschutes River between the boat ramps at Trout Creek Campground and Harpham Flat near Maupin, a thirty four-mile stretch usually taken in three days. For those who haven't, this is a place of singular intensity; a roaring, seething, boat-eating cauldron. And there's no going around it. If you want to drift that stretch of river -and you should- you will need to get through it. Depending on what map you read, Whitehorse is either a class 3-plus or 4 piece of water. Regardless of how it's categorized, it is all you'd ever want in a drift boat, which is the only way I know it.

Several years ago I saw the rapid for the first time from the scouting point. We were on a group "Shake-Down" float with all the guides and employees of Fly and Field Outfitters, the fly shop I'd recently joined here in Bend. That day, after rowing straight to the rapid, there were a bunch of us milling nervously about on a bluff above the river. My chauffeur was being instructed by a much more experienced oarsman on the finer points of how to enter, navigate and ultimately find your way to the bottom of the initial, harrowing drop. It was only his second time down the rapid. We had spent the day till that point rowing from Trout Creek as the river wasn't open to fishing yet. I felt the mounting nerves from the rowers seat. Having never seen the rapid, I wasn't sure what the fuss was about. But standing there, scanning the massive chaotic torrent, I understood. What ended up happening was a less than textbook run, me trying to remain calm as one of the rocks meant to pass on our port side raced by on starboard, the intrepid oarsman grappling to find a way to safety. Although we made it through intact, the run would prove to leave a lasting impression.

The next year found me approaching the rapid in my own drift boat, *Ruby Redside*, psyched to get a first run under my belt, a good friend and massively skilled oarsman leading in a raft. The morning of our second day we stopped at the scouting pullout and wandered down to the point above the heart of the rapid where the full roar of water compels every sense. That's where I froze. Even now I'm not ashamed to admit that. As I scanned the rapid, top to bottom, examining each visible rock, each tumbling wave, each arching, distorted hydraulic, my mind raced over the various scenarios, every potential outcome, good *and* bad. Then a horrible vision filled my imagination. There's a video I saw once when my fascination with Whitehorse was fresh and new. It was easily found on YouTube. The video is shot from below the worst part of the rapid, one rafter filming his buddy following in another raft. But the guy with the camera notices a drift boat entering the rapid, obviously in immediate and acute trouble, and averts focus to it. In the next 10 seconds the hapless rower digs pathetically at the frothing caps of waves and then simply clouts the first big rock, "Can Opener". In the blink of an eye the boat is upside down, occupants and every piece of gear is distributed into the angry waters. It is a yard sale of coolers, dry bags, fishing gear and people. An instant later the video ends, presumably so the shooter could begin attempting to salvage gear and retrieve people.

I only watched the video once. The nightmares occurred for months. I couldn't erase the vision from my memory. Every time I imagined myself rowing the rapid, I saw the wreck, over and over. Sure, I located and studied videos of perfect runs. I watched people stick it at 4000cfs, 6000, 7800. I watched hand held "bow cam" runs, Go Pro cams mounted above the rower's seat, excited onlookers' videos shot from the railroad tracks. Movie after movie showed me exactly how to do it. My friends and co-workers encouraged me. My bosses impressed upon me how important it was that I get down there and row my boat the length of the river. I told myself over and over that I could do it. Then Whitehorse and I came face-to-face. And I froze. It wasn't long before my friend Chris realized my state. He asked, caring and casual, "How you feeling, man?"

"Not so hot," I replied, staring at the growling river.

"What do you want to do?" he asked, without any sense of urging.

"I dunno," I said, shaking my head, trying to clear the bad images, trying to conjure good ones. Silently, I asked the river if it was my turn. Over the roar of cascading water, over the doubts echoing in the canyon of my psyche, the river emphatically said *No*. I finally turned to him, "I don't think I'm good for this."

"Alright, cool," he said without even a hint of disappointment. Then we turned and went up the steep trail to where our friends waited. After one last look from above I turned and said, "Yea man, not feeling it."

"Let's go down in my raft," Chris announced. "Then if you want, we can go in *Ruby* with either me or you rowing."

We told the other guys our plan and went up to Chris' raft. After shoving off from the scouting beach, we had at least a hundred yards of broad, almost hushed river before the rapid began. There are boulders out there that create seam lines. Chris had shown them to me from up on the railroad tracks. They were obvious from up there. From river level they weren't. I was suddenly relieved with my decision. Following him through was the original idea, but the previous day, when running some much easier water I had lost track of his positions a few times. Seeing someone's line can be very deceiving from behind when both boats are moving. Not to mention Chris was rowing a large, framed raft and I was in a drift boat; two very different vessels. So as I sat in the front of his raft that morning, I tried to scan for landmarks, hummocks, electrical poles along the railroad, boulders and water features, anything that might help lead the way when alone. It is well known that entry position is everything when rowing big water. You need to be in very specific places, going very specific speeds at very specific angles. There are lots of ways to screw up rowing rapids, but entering the wrong way is usually certain failure. Whitehorse is no different; actually it is perhaps the most precise drift boat entry you'll ever see.

And then we were above the tumult. As Chris rowed, he talked me through every oar stroke, every ferry angle, every indication that the boat was in the right place, aimed the right way, going the right speed. It was by all accounts a perfect, effortless run. After pulling the raft in below "House Rock" we walked along the tracks, up to the bluff above the entrance to the rapid and stopped there, our friends a respectful distance, Chris letting me assess. I asked again of the river *is today my time*. The river, unblinking, without sympathy, in a whispered roar said *HELL NO!* To Chris' credit, he didn't even portray a trace of disenchantment. We simply walked up, got in *Ruby* and he ran it again, perfectly. I shot video of this run on my cell phone from the client's seat. The footage is blurry because the lens focuses on rods, not the water. But the angles are there, the ferry positions, the calm, stress-less strokes. The minute we pulled in at "House Rock", as the adrenalin dissipated, I felt massive sorrow and chagrin at having passed up my first chance to row the 'horse. Those emotions would stay with me for the next year, haunting, causing a tightening in the chest.

This last spring the demons were exorcized. The same crew from the previous trip was there with the addition of a fellow guide, Sterling, who had also never rowed the rapid. We camped above Whitehorse and spent much of the previous day and night talking about what awaited us. Sterling and I were both nervous, but feeling as if it was our time; we had put in the hours, knew our boats, were respectful of our task, reverent of the consequences, but ready. For me, the walk down to scout was cursory; I had thought about it so much and watched so many videos. I knew what I wanted to do and, if I'm honest, I didn't want the river to talk me out of it again. Sterling was having a harder time processing. He and Chris spent a while going over entry position and angle, what to do once you're in the rapid, things to avoid, ways to get out of bad situations. I finally told Chris that I needed to get it done; no more waiting. I checked in with Sterling and immediately recognized the state he was in. The doubt and fear were being inflated every second he stood there staring at the cacophonic violence. I suggested that instead of following us, Sterling and our buddy Amato could hang back and watch, then Chris would come back and run it in the front of Sterling's boat, coaching him through. That idea appealed and was agreed to right away. Based on everything you've read so far, you have to know that I empathized with Sterling. I understood how he felt, from the dryness in his mouth to the cramping in his stomach, the difficulty in processing deep breaths. So I was in no way pushing him to do something he wasn't ready to do, especially in his new boat. But I also knew not going then and there would have been much harder for him to live with.

So with the new plan hatched, Sterling wished me luck and then went to watch my run from a vantage a little ways downriver. The walk back up to the boat was calm. Chris gave me space, but was no doubt gauging my condition. He's known me long enough and been through enough with me to have a sense. Our dear friend, Travis, would join us. He walked a few steps behind, allowing Chris and I our time in those last few minutes before climbing aboard *Ruby* and going. Chris asked just before the steep trail to the boats, "You good, brother?"

"Yea, man." And then I turned to him. "Solid. Thanks, bro."

As we put on lifejackets I guzzled water and tried to calm myself. The nerves were coming in waves, swelling, dispersing, then revisiting anew. They wouldn't go away. That much I knew. I had a flashback to the sensations I felt while getting strapped into a Formula Ford racecar. The first twenty times there was always the same rushing of nervous energy. I learned to embrace it, channel and harness. On this day, as we rowed away from the scouting beach and began the slow, quiet drift down, I allowed my vision to scan towering caldera bluffs, canyon rims, the shapes of clouds, an osprey standing sentinel atop a tree along the far left bank. Chris and Travis spoke casually in the front. Deep breathes and a brief, sincere invocation of the river to humor our presence.

Chris gave calm encouragement as the roar of the river began intruding. The seam we'd focused on from above was harder to locate at water level. But once we were on it, Chris was amazing at coaching which oar to use and how hard to use it. Then we were there, way passed the point of no return, at last properly engulfed in Whitehorse.

As a quick aside, it should be noted that Whitehorse Rapid, like all the famous stretches of whitewater, has a handful of named rocks. To briefly introduce: The "Knuckles" are at the top and can either be ferried in behind or pushed between. "Hog's Back" is right behind the "Knuckles" and rarely comes into play but has claimed many boats. "Plug Rock" is subsurface and doesn't even register until the river is around 4000cfs. "Can Opener" is the really bad one. It's been a magnet for uncountable boats. It is also a navigational moment in every run that must be made in a short window of time.

"Oh Shit" is named because if you're worried about it, you're in trouble whether you hit it or not. The "Reef" encroaches on the left just below "Oh Shit" and has a heavy current coming off, pushing you into the nastiness on your right. The "Boulder Garden" is just that. The last two-thirds of the run are adjacent this area. It is a field of big enough rocks that any one of them could bury a gunnel or bend a boat. Above 6000cfs they are mostly submerged enough to go over. Mostly. The "Washing Machine" is not so much an avoidable obstruction as a series of standing waves, a derangement, a liquid convulsion, entirely unpredictable. Those are the important landmarks. Now let's have a go...

Chris's last instructions were to give a couple positive strokes as we ferried in just behind "The Knuckles". From that point he only complimented what I was doing. Once committed and in the right spot, my thinking slowed to an almost clinical speed. Get the stern over the left "Knuckle" with the correct ferry angle, still backing slightly into the eddy. Steady the boat as she moves slowly towards "Humpback". Skid the bottom of the transom over "Plug Rock" ("the sound of safety") pointing the bow straight at "Can Opener". This is where every oar stroke becomes critical. No matter how heavy the situation feels, every stroke must be compact, meaningful, without panic. Now the river is pushing straight at "Can Opener" and I put in a couple really positive strokes to stay off *that* nasty, destructive rock. The tricky part of this zone is that the boat must get really close to the rock so as to stay off the quickly encroaching "Boulder Garden". Then, just as the bow is clear of "Can Opener" rotate quickly so that the boat is now facing the river right bank and then pull off the seam pushing hard towards the chaotic "Boulder Garden" only a boat's length away. A couple more stout backstrokes into the eddy then release the bow down river. This is where it gets steep and fast. Hold the boat straight downriver with the "Reef" ripping passed on the port side, the "Boulder Garden" on starboard. The "Washing Machine" awaits now, big waves crossing, bulging, and collapsing randomly. Micro strokes to keep the boat's direction and speed in check. There is no way of knowing what the waves will do. Hold the correct angle and just drop in, hoping for the best. On this run the boat did what she was meant to do, what she was built for. It was a remarkably dry run through the "Washing Machine". And once into the relatively calm water below the torrent I let out a great, high-pitched war hoop, releasing year's worth of anxiety from my winded lungs. The boys took turns facing me, offering congratulatory knuckles.

We pulled in behind "House Rock" and dropped anchor. Beers were extracted from the cooler, opened, used to "cheers" with and imbibed. Chris and Travis were cool in how they praised the run and felt a huge stoke for me. No two guys I'd rather have shared *that* beer with. I was just floating...really no other way to describe it. There was simply weightlessness. The wind's caress felt indescribably good. A bead of sweat trickled from under my hat, across my temple, to my ear. But mostly there was the sensation of a very large, very heavy monkey having been lifted from my back. It was a pretty good feeling.

The three of us made our way up the riprap bank and began walking along the tracks. I honestly don't remember much of that time. I do know that I was internally debriefing intensely for the next half-hour or so. I went back over every aspect of the run, trying to program as much as I could.

Travis and I picked a spot to stop and watch Sterling's run. Chris went ahead a couple hundred yards and met those guys up by the scouting bluff. They stood there for maybe five long minutes. I could practically *feel* Sterling's nerves from where we stood. Then they began walking up towards the boat and vanished.

The pullout for Whitehorse is quite a ways upriver from where you actually scout. When you're about to row, whether walking back and forth or standing at the top, time sort of flies by while standing still. From below, while waiting for your buddy, who you know is going through hell right then, it seems an eternity from the time they disappear, till the boat appears for the last thirty seconds before dropping into the rapid. Travis and I hung out talking about the day and the fishing and how awesome our trip had been up to that point. But it seemed we waited for a long time before we saw those guys again.

Then there they were. Perfect position on the seam, pointed at the river left bank, drifting from left to right just a little. Sterling put good strokes on it just over the left "Knuckle" and bobbed in the eddy momentarily. Then the boat just absolutely shot left. It must have caught an especially turbulent seam coming off the "Knuckles" and was posthaste darting over the top of "Can Opener". From our vantage point it looked as if a tiny toy boat was being dragged into the worst possible spot be some unseen and especially malevolent child. Sterling's strokes took on a little more urgency at that point, but the boat's momentum was holding it above the rock and now drifting towards it. Both Travis and I beseeched of him to get back enough to clear the rock. The "Can Opener" has claimed dozens, if not hundreds of boats over the years and now I know why. Eventually Chris leaned back and pretty much barked at Sterling to get some strokes in and move the boat backwards. When that finally happened, they were riding the seam off the top of "Can Opener" and towards the "Boulder Garden", pointed the wrong direction. They remained at a slight ferry angle, pointed down and towards river left long after there should have been a one hundred and twenty-degree shift to river right. Sterling was digging to rotate the boat, but once amongst the boulders there's nothing but wave tops and whitewater, neither of which produce much purchase. He dug with a heavier rhythm for several long seconds. Eventually the oars bit in hard on one rotation stroke and the boat spun. Then it kept spinning. I don't know if he put in another stroke or if the river was just producing nightmare fodder. But in the blink of an eye he had the stern facing down river. He had gotten off the "Boulder Garden" but was now heading towards the "Washing Machine". Backwards.

Then they disappeared behind some trees.

I will admit now that I half expected to see them next in the vicinity of "House Rock", a swamped boat, gear bobbing impatiently in the eddy or continuing its way towards to Columbia, a mad scramble to save whatever we could. But no, that is not what happened. What happened is that Sterling got through, somehow. Backwards.

If you talk to any of the experienced guides who work on the Lower Decshutes, they will all tell you that there are two kinds of guides working the "Camp Stretch", those who *have* shit their pants in Whitehorse, and those who *will* shit their pants in Whitehorse. Sterling got his diaper-filling run out of the way first time through. You wouldn't have known that talking to him right after. I mean I knew he was a bit shaken, but the kid has a cool, quiet confidence to him that shone through even then. It is something that quite simply cannot be taught. By the time we got down to them that morning he was sipping a brew, smiling, chuckling the nerves off his shoulder like a Salmonfly. We didn't talk about it then, but I could feel his heart racing the whole time. And if I'm to be totally honest, mine hadn't slowed significantly in over an hour.

I could have named this story, "The Day I Almost Punched a Client in the Face". That title would undoubtedly have raised eyebrows, gotten more reads, and vaulted me into a higher echelon of fly-fishing authors. But I don't need that kind of attention. I will, though, tell you now why it could have been named so.

A couple weeks after the boy's trip I was back down they're with clients for the first time. It was a fully supported, four-person camp trip during the famed Salmonfly hatch. My fellow guide, Kevin and I each had a couple guys in our boats and the legendary Dave was bagging. It was by all accounts the "A" Team, except for me. We enjoyed amazing fishing the first day. But I was having a hard time getting much pleasure out of it. No matter how many fish clobbered the Chubby Chernobyl, how perfect the weather was or how good *Ruby* felt, my mind constantly raced out ahead of us, to the rapid we'd take on day two. That night we were treated to an all-time meal of massive steaks and even bigger lobster tails brought by one of the clients. It was next-level extravagance. There was beer and wine and jokes and story telling, and I barely enjoyed a second of it. Far earlier than normal I slunk off to my tent to read.

In the morning Dave and I whipped up some mega breakfast burritos and then everyone hurriedly broke down camp. Once the boats were stowed, Kevin, Dave and I agreed that we'd "social float" to the rapid, scout it, and run as a team. I loved the idea of the three of us scouting together. Both those boys have run it hundreds of times. There was the added element that we'd heard of a drift boat hung up somewhere in the rapid, and that Mark Angel, the only guy permitted to salvage such situations, might be there that morning trying to extract it. And so it was set. We'd casually row the mile or so down, pull in and go for a little walk. The clients could either walk with us or stick around the boats and fish. Ten minutes into the float Kevin pulled over to fish his guys off one of the islands. My stomach tightened. Already a deviation from the plan. Not ideal. I rowed up next to Dave and we drifted along for a few more minutes. Just above the pullout for scouting I watched as he pulled his lifejacket on. "Hey, Dave. Whatcha doin'?"

"Oh, think I'm just gonna go for it..."

Shit. Really? "What if Mark's in there?"

"He usually puts a sign down here at the beach," he replied way too casually.

Usually, huh? "Uh, okay. Cool." I was trying to sound unfazed as my clients looked back at me. "I'll pull over and run down there to make sure."

"No need," he said. "Should be fine."

Should be fine?

As we approached the pullout I pointed to a tree-shaded bank area and told the clients to go back up and fish once anchored. Then we pulled in; I jumped out and trotted down to where I could see the top of the rapid. I got there just in time to watch Dave drop in. It was really cool to see his technique; so calm and smooth, even in a drift boat laden down with tons of gear. He stuck the run, unsurprisingly, and then was gone. Only then did it occur to me to look for the allegedly stranded boat. I scanned the rapid and at first didn't see anything. Then my focus was drawn to something down there, amongst the chaos of glistening explosions. Yup, there, on top of "Can Opener", waving grotesquely above the seething torrent was a lone oar handle. It was swaying slowly side to side as if still trying to save the run; maybe one more good stroke and it would be okay. But it wasn't okay. Not even a little. It was hideous, horror movie-esque, a vulgar vision. And yet I couldn't avert my stare. Then I noticed that what first appeared to be the rock was actually a drift boat having become a mangled, folded perversion of its once proud self, which was now thoroughly pinned upriver of "Can Opener". The oar had somehow remained in its lock, blade down. The pillow in the current between the boat and the rock was holding the blade almost softly, allowing it to move ever so slightly left to right, right to left, over and over and over. I stared for another minute, reached into my shirt pocket for a smoke and then spent a solid minute trying to produce fire with a perfectly functioning lighter, so violently my fingers trembled.

On the walk back up to *Ruby* I kept shaking my head, trying to erase the vision, trying ineptly to not imagine what had happened to that boat and the guys who had been in it two days before. These are the times that my vivid, hyper-drive imagination is a most unwelcome thing, because little of it is actually required most of the time, yet way more often than I'd prefer, it goes into practically microscopic detail. So in an attempt to distract myself, I closed and reopened eyes, kicked the random rock, scanned the far bank for a bald eagle, took another drag from the smoke. Nope. Didn't work. The entire sequence played itself out in my head; from the initial moment of terror, that exact instant of knowing the run had gone unavoidably wrong; the ensuing collision with an utterly stationary rock; the sound of the boat, that cherished steed, as she collapsed; the emptying of gear, much of it no doubt precious, into the river; the shocking cold of the springtime Deschutes and weight of her currents; the frantic attempt at swimming to a safe eddy, wondering what's become of your boat mates; the realization that life has been dramatically and forever altered for the worse; all of it seen with far too much clarity. Damned imagination. Oh to be a simpleton. Why can't I just gaze upon the destruction, conceive of the lives thrown into terror and disarray, and think, *Well, shit. They sure screwed that one up. Alrighty then, let's do this!* Yea, no, I can't do that.

Once back up at *Ruby*, with no sign of Kevin, and my clients still around the corner, I took a minute to re-rig a nymph rod. Then, just to, you know, make sure it was sound, I caught a beautiful 16" Redband right in front of the boat. Even as I was playing and landing the fish my mind wandered downriver and all I really wanted, what appealed to me more than anything in the entire world, I wanted to be Dave. I wanted to be somewhere down around Davidson Camp, oar handles tucked under knees, my only concern figuring out what music to listen to.

It would be another 20 minutes before Kevin rowed around the corner and pulled in. "Hey there, fellah!" he chirped. "Whatcha doin'?"

"Waiting for you," I said, trying not to sound too perturbed. "My guys on their way down?"

"Yup. Said they caught a bunch of fish under those trees. Nice call." The compliment may have been an attempt at easing my poorly veiled displeasure with him for not sticking with the set plan. As he got out of his boat, he said, "Let's go down and scout."

"Already did. Ready to go," I replied, unconvincingly.

"Aw, come on! It'll be fun."

The clients stayed back. Kevin and I walked down there in, as I recall, total silence. We stopped right around where I had been earlier. I let Kevin scan the rapid.

"Oh dude!" he exclaimed when he saw the oar handle. "That's gnarly!" I didn't respond. "Let's go down there where we can see it better."

"Nope. I've seen enough."

"Yea, yea. Cool." We stood for a moment. "You want to go first or follow," he asked.

"I'll follow."

"Yea, for sure. So listen, if anything goes wrong..."

"Stop talking!" I half barked. Then a bit more timidly, "I'm good. Let's go."

"Yea, you're right," he began. "I'm over-thinking as usual."

"*Think* all you want," I said, trying to lighten the mood. "Just stop *talking*."

By the time we got back to the boats all four clients were milling about. None of them knew what was around the corner. We'd only told them that there was some "whitewater" that morning. A few minutes were spent stowing the anchor and other gear, making sure nothing was likely to fall off, and me swigging water. We all got our lifejackets on and set off down river. I pulled hard on the oars a couple times to get us in some current, looked up beyond the craggy basalt and into the sparkling blue sky. Then I murmured inwardly, *seems as good a day as any to die.* I actually thought that. And you know what, it calmed me, made me smile and be grateful for everything and everyone that's come before that exact instant in time.

I let Kevin get quite a ways in front, not knowing how much he'd slow just prior to the "Knuckles". Then I instructed, quite spontaneously, for the clients to not speak until they were told they could and set about looking for the seam, you know, *that* seam, the one I *had* to be on. For an instant all the boulders looked the same. Every crease in the otherwise flat river was anonymous. I was lost. There were perhaps fifteen seconds of abject confusion. The boat was definitely pointed in the right direction. That much I knew. Kevin, until then my vague reference as to where I should be, had dropped in and was bobbing amidst the tumult. But where was I? Then it occurred to me that I was about ten feet right of where I needed to be. A decision had to be made. Push hard, try to get over to the seam, and risk entering with too much speed? Or rotate the bow to river right, pull back and then re-rotate, hoping I was stationed on the correct line right when I had to pull back over the left "Knuckle"? Or just jump the hell off and swim for the bank? I opted for Plan "B". I'd love to see how much my heart rate spiked right then. It was a massive moment of recovery. As it was, I ferried in behind the "Knuckles", rode the seam towards "Can Opener", spun her back at the right time and then flew down into the "Washing Machine", taking one pretty good wave over the starboard gunnel. Once through the wave train one of my clients spun to me, wild eyed. He obviously wanted to say something. "Oh, crap! I forgot. Yea, you can talk now," I chirped.

"Oh, Jesus! Did you see the boat hung up on that rock? That was crazy!"

"Yea," I lied. In all truthfulness, in the moment I had no recollection of seeing the boat while rowing. I'm guessing that means my focus was so acute, so unflinching that the wreck really didn't register. That, or I had closed my eyes and was just randomly rowing, hoping for the best.

We pulled in and anchored a ways downriver. Kevin's guys were standing on the bank, having cracked their breakfast beers, yucking it up. After giving Kevin a hug, I reached into our cooler and pulled out a beer. I don't drink when guiding. Except right then and right there. Yup, just made up a new rule. I opened the beer, took a long swig, poured some into the river and then saluted the guys. The dude who had booked the trip, looked at me for a second and said, "Shit, Griff. Your hand's shaking. What're you scared or something?"

I looked over at him and replied, trying to remain calm, "Just a little adrenalin."

He wasn't through, "Damn, it ain't that heavy," there was some next-level D-bag in his voice.

"I'd like to see you do it," was my reply, and I immediately wished I could put the words back from whence they'd come.

"Seriously?!!!" he belched. Yea, my challenge hadn't gone over so well. "Drag a boat back up there! I'll row that shit right now!!" As the ridiculousness of his words and the assholeness in their meaning swam in the rapids of my brain, I turned away from him and towards the river. It took me a minute to smile; just long enough for the image of me punching him in his smug face to dance gleefully out over the water. I know, I know, the story would be so much better if I DID punch him in the face. And go ahead; let your imagination see it happening. See the ensuing scuffle, clients and Kevin pulling me off the crumpled, bloody heap after I'd landed a half-dozen additional adrenaline-addled blows. Imagine the rest of that day with the arrogant, ungrateful asshole pressing ice to his swollen left eye and dealing with the recurring nosebleeds. Then imagine how that all might have affected my tip. I know, that was a really fun exercise right up until then.

As it was, I took one more loving draught from my beer and poured the rest into the river. The remainder of the trip went great. And I got a fat tip.

Fast forward to last weekend. We were on a six-boat flotilla, 17 people strong. Again drifting from Trout Creek down to Maupin. The reason for this trip was to be present for a wedding taking place two-thirds of the way down. My good buddy Dave (yes he of legend from the last trip) was marrying the dearest Suzanne. Theirs is a special bond, one of those rare occasions when you'd have to accuse the universe of callous neglect if they hadn't crossed paths where and when they did. The wedding was fairly impromptu and casual. But it would happen in the majestic depths of the Deschutes canyon first weekend of August, during the sweltering Dog Days of summer. Me and mine were honored to be included.

As for Whitehorse, well it would be another first for me: my wife and 21 year-old son, Jasper would be positioned in the front of *Ruby* for the entire three-day adventure. This would be Michelie's first exposure to my work place and Jasper's first experience in the "Camp Stretch". For many weeks leading up to the trip every time I conjured the image of the three of us dropping in to the rapid caused a quickening of my pulse. They've both heard about the heaviness of the place. How horrifying would it be if this run went wrong? How awful would I feel if I put two of my favorite people through an ordeal down there in the unforgiving canyon?

The first day was all fun, some fishing, much social floating, a few beers, the occasional water fight and then camp. We had the lower site at Whisky Dick, the one on the big eddy around the bend from all the others. The afternoon was spent with all of us sitting in camp chairs on the sandbar in the eddy, knee-deep, simply rolling into the river from time to time to cool off. The day lingered into a pleasant afternoon and evening. Some of us fished the caddis into darkness. We all ate a great meal amongst great laughter. Most everyone vanished into tents before it got too late. This was a veteran crew, knowing the next day required some modicum of alertness and the next night we'd all get a little crazier. Maybe a lot...

In the morning, with Whitehorse looming just a mile downriver, I couldn't eat, coffee tasted nasty, the sun shone way too bright, no camp jokes were especially funny. I broke down camp, then Jasper and I packed *Ruby*. He and Michelie were both respectfully calm, both fully understanding where my head was. Once the boats were stowed and ready to head down to the scouting beach I suddenly had the irrevocable need to evacuate my bowels, which given the popularity of the outhouse at Whisky Dick that morning was next level unpleasant. But those moments, alone and determined, girding for what lay ahead, breathing only through my mouth, proved to be what I needed.

On the casual float to Whitehorse I pulled alongside my buddy Curtis. He was with his girlfriend and dog, along to both hang out as well as bag a bunch of random gear. He's rowed down there quite a lot. Without conferring with my boat mates, I inquired, "Hey, Curtis. You planning on scouting?"

He smiled over and said, "Not really. I don't like scouting this thing."

That was all I needed to hear. We would deviate from the plan and just go. Life jackets were donned, I guzzled a Gatorade and made sure the boat was sound. Everything was ready to go. I only had to pull the anchor in over the transom and we were set. Then the river bent right. The scouting beaches were there, then gone. I looked back and saw Kevin peering down river at us; no doubt bummed we hadn't stopped. I instructed my wife and kid to remain silent until we were through the worst. Individually, they looked back with smiles. Jasper's was full of encouragement, confident in his Papa. Michelie's had a little more concern. I just smiled back at her and nodded. Then Curtis showed me the seam I needed to be on. We glided in.

This run had new elements, but was every bit as intense. I've already labored over the machinations of the run. Now I'll try to relate the inward experience. It's hard to describe what it feels like once the rapid has fully engulfed you. And now that I think about it, I'm not really sure how much of the actual event is processed. But for sure every one of my senses is assaulted, every synapse fires. All around there is movement. Great forces tug menacingly, sometimes is different directions from one side of the boat to the other. Water in every conceivable river hue bounces, rushing, beautiful, horrific. I suddenly feel as small and insignificant as I ever have. The reality that the river doesn't care occurs to me. But in this abject chaos there is the simple reality that I can't blow it; the stakes are too high. Amidst a barrage of tiny question marks, I focus on making short, positive, meaningful strokes. Within this flurry of uncontrollable elements, I try to stay one step ahead of the river for this brief, awkward dance. At some point I realize that the worst is behind me. Then I give hearty thanks to the river goddess for humoring my intrusion one more time. I silently offer an invocation to those I love that they might someday understand what the moment means in my very core. Then I pull in behind "House Rock" and crack open a beer.

I should report that this run had been my smoothest yet in terms of fewest strokes and positioning of the boat. I actually spoke a couple times: first to let them both know that the scraping of the transom on "Plug Rock" was a good thing, and then to tell them how good *Ruby* felt for those most critical strokes to tuck in behind "Can Opener". The look of relief and elation was impressed on them both when the last wave was behind us.

In the case of last weekend, Jasper and I scrambled up the bank and watched several boats make their way down the rapid. Every time I get to watch someone else row Whitehorse I feel a slightly deeper understanding of her energy, her currents, the infinite and ephemeral textures of water and the boldness of her intensity. On this day I got to watch guys I've known and respected for years run it. I got to watch buddies take the run for their first time. I watched some perfect runs and some not quite so. At every boat we howled encouragingly. I took many pictures. Most are blurry because my hands were still shaking slightly. The adrenalin takes a while to subside.

I'm still haunted some nights by visions of how poorly things can go down there. I'm reminded by oarsmen far more experienced than myself of the uncaring fluctuations in Whitehorse's currents. I hear stories all the time about how so-and-so wrecked their boat in the rapid and quit guiding because of it. I get sent links to YouTube videos of hapless people who ventured into the canyon only to be spat out in particulate matter, all their belongings now littering the majestic river's bottom. I dream about her beauty, her violence, her seduction and lightening quick retribution for misbehavior or poor judgment. I long to feel her currents pulling on me. I'm not sure I've ever felt such an undeniable adoration and unequivocal fear of any one thing. And yet even now as I write this, even as you sit reading it, she's down there roaring. And she couldn't give a damn if you hear it.

Chapter 15

The Autumnal Romance

Winter

I think all us anglers, whether recreational or professional, tend to break up calendar years based on seasons and hatches, or rivers flows and drainage fishability. For some that's as simple as broad stroking each of the four seasons. For others it's as complex and thorough as weekly hatch predictions, complete with what hours of the day should be spent fishing and which hours are for golf. Some of us have one or two rivers that we focus on primarily throughout the year. Some have destinations we plan annually based on past experience or legend. But no matter our particular attention to the seasons or months, there is undoubtedly a special span of time we look forward to every year. For many years now, that has been the month of October for me. Before my career as a full-time professional guide, I always set chunks of time for my own fishing travels. I've long lost count of days on the McCloud River in Northern California hiking the wild canyon amongst moist, fallen leaves, wisps of clouds clinging to towering pine-covered walls, golden-hued "Elephant Ears" drooping to the river's surface, casting large caddis imitations over chunky native rainbows. Most of these trips were solo adventures, my trusted, bad-ass yellow lab, Satchel there every step. I had fishing buddies that would occasionally join, but truth be told I wanted the solitude. I craved the time to appreciate what the entire trout season had allowed me. I'd spend long hours by the fire after fortifying meals, with the dog snoozing at my feet, catching up my fishing journals from scattered notepads full of ridiculous details.

And now that I guide twelve months of the year, the concept of a favorite time is even more elusive. Yet somehow, even as I write this, during the shortest days of the year, my mind races ahead to October 2016.

Or back to the 10th month of 2015.

In all of the thirty or so Octobers I've fly fished, this last one was about as fun, varied and fulfilling as any. As sad as it is to report, this story was not written by a campfire along the banks of the McCloud with Satchel nearby. She is no longer with us and I now longer call the California river "home". This story is written here, in my shambles of a writing den, an impatient Australian Shepherd just outside the door, wondering when we'll go fishing next. Soon, Eddy. Soon.

October saw us as busy on the Lower Deschutes as we've been all season. In a rather unexpected burst of activity we had guides working from Warm Springs down to the waters around Maupin, including several memorable multi-day trips. Now, as deepest winter envelops, I feel compelled to reflect for a moment on what an amazing 10th month we had.

Early in the month I had the pleasure of guiding one of my favorite people I've met on the big river. Steve is a guy from New Jersey who lived in these parts a decade and a half ago. He now owns crazy popular coffee shops called Green Planet Coffee Company, not far from New York City in New Jersey. Twice a year he visits Oregon and rents the house down at Luelling Homestead. For those of you unfamiliar with the property, it is the upstream-most homestead on the 100 miles of the Lower Deschutes. It has been for sale for a couple years and still gets rented out nowadays to people like Steve. I've rowed passed more times than I can count. I've fished along the riverfront property with great success many times. But I'd never had the offer to stay there. That would change this year. Steve and I negotiated a two-day trip that had us fish down to the property one day and then to the Trout Creek ramp the next.

But first, a bit of history. My first encounter with Steve was *last* October. I had just turned fifty and was on a quest for the first steelhead of my sixth decade. Eddy and I were doing the "Day Stretch", just me and the dog, a Spey rod, a big single-hander and the volition to touch some steel. It was at the first stop, "Car Bar" when I realized I'd forgotten my tip wallet. For whatever reason it was in a backpack I'd left in the truck. So very early in the day I was resigned to casting bobber rigs, which normally I'd be cool with, but on this day I was so psyched to swing with the two-hander, not to mention my tennis elbow was pretty bad. For anyone who has suffered this ailment you know that roll casting and mending line are especially painful. The dog and I made our way down to Luelling Bar where I fooled a couple really nice trout under the bobber. The wind was picking up into the late morning, blowing downriver. After pulling anchor and beginning to drift, I looked over at the homestead and saw a guy sitting on a plastic lawn chair near the river's edge. I'd thought of stopping to fish the bucket below the riffle but figured the guy was just resting the water. As we drifted passed I noticed he was drinking coffee and having a smoke. I hollered over, "Mornin'! How are ya?"

The guy stood to respond. "Good! How's the fishin'?"

"Oh, pretty good," I said, as a standard reply. My attention, though was focused on that sweet drop off I knew he hadn't touched

"Cool dog. She likes fishing with you?"

"You know... Better than a day at home."

"You want to fish here? I'm done. Taking off in a few."

I didn't need any further tempting. A minute later the anchor was down, me having taken the long way under the shade tree so as not to spook any fish. "Bring your dog up. It's all good."

Eddy and I hopped ashore and made our way up to our new friend. After introductions, we talked fishing for a while. He had been down there for a week renting the house and hosting friends. He told me that he'd gotten a few steelhead fishing the property water. Everyone had left the day before and he was getting ready to hit the road for the airport soon.

There was something immediately likable with Steve. Aside from the overt and sincere friendliness, he also possessed a certain zeal for life, there was passion in every word, every gesture. Not to mention he looked like a retired rock star or producer. And he had that quality most interesting to me as both a man and an angler; he was *interested*!

As it was, I didn't even fish the bucket that day. It was so nice hanging out with Steve, playing with Eddy, we had a cup of coffee and a smoke. The wind built under a grey sky. So in the end, the dog and I jumped back in *Ruby* and continued our leisurely float. No steelhead were caught that day.

Fast-forward to this last June, late in the month, engulfed in an oppressive heat, the caddis hatch blowing up. I had a couple clients with me and as we pulled in under the shade tree I looked up at the house and saw a guy on the porch. Even from that distance, I recognized him as Steve, so I yelled up. He came to the river, offering cold beers, handshakes and hugs. I was working so there wasn't much chitchat. Steve did hang out to witness a truly giant trout hooked inches from the bank right behind the boat. We didn't land that one, but he was so genuinely excited for me and my client that we'd even touched such a fish. He'd had really slow fishing for a few days and was just stoked to see some action. We did speak that day about his fall trip and how he might like to hire me for a day or two. I gave him the standard, "Better book soon. That's a really busy time for me," response.

Fast-forward again to mid-September. A text comes in. Can I guide Steve and friends for a couple days early October? Naturally I was already booked. In subsequent texts he starts juicing up the pot. "Stay the night at the Homestead." "Awesome dinner." "Great wine." "Best pal in the world is coming." "Big cash tip." Well, hell Steve. Why didn't you say so? Things got moved around. The dates were booked. And I was properly looking forward to it.

Boy, that was some preamble.

This year Steve brought his lovely wife Patty and a few other friends from places dotted across the country. I met them at the Warm Springs boat ramp in the afternoon. In the boat would be Steve, Patty and their good pal, Reggie. Both Patty and Reggie were new to the fly-fishing thing. We fished lazily down to the homestead, stopping at a few of my favorite spots. Things didn't go especially great with Patty and I right away. She got with the program quickly enough and in no time hooked a really nice trout. The fish ran and jumped and I thought for sure it would shake free. Somehow she maintained contact, but when it came down to the fight, she was messing up pretty badly. I fully understand how counter-intuitive elements of fly fishing can be, but she was just flailing. So eventually I raised my voice a little, you know, for emphasis. It's what I do. I think my increased volume would have been okay but for Steve wading down and trying to coach her at the same time. Basically it was shit show. One of those circus carnival moments when you just want to teleport anywhere other than where you are. Patty was awesome. Through the chaos, she screamed, "Stop yelling at me!" A minute later we had the fish in the net. We took some pictures and then set it free. We high-fived. I tried to diffuse the situation. We went over the "do's and don'ts" of playing fish for future reference. Then went back to fishing. I thought we were cool. We weren't.

I think we only stopped three or four times that afternoon. No steelhead were landed, but some awfully beautiful trout were. My usual nymph combos were effective as long they were drifted the right way through the right water. Fortunately these three were more than up to the task. It was a lovely afternoon that eased into an even nicer evening, culminating on the Luelling Bar across from the house. This is a favorite spot for many of us on that stretch of river. It's basically the bottom section of a massive gravel bar. The upper stretches are prime spawning grounds. And the pool above has some epic redds. The section we fish is right before it drops off into pretty turbulent water. Depending on what part of the bar you're fishing, you might be anywhere from ten feet to one step away from fast, confused and deep currents. The cast is not easy from the lower bar, but if you set you rig up right, make a decent cast and then feed line, you will fool fish. I took Reggie down there while Steve fished above. Just briefly, a little about Reggie. He's a big, strong, East Coast kinda guy from Jersey. No doubt busted some heads in his day. Caught all kinds of big freakin' fish in the ocean on gear. Owns the biggest nightclub in the state. Doesn't get told what to do much, if you get my meaning. But he didn't know shit about fooling trout with a fly rod. He had, up until then, hooked some nice ones. But he had the tendency to walk backwards after hooking a fish instead of stripping line in. Even on false set, he would immediately start moving. We call it "Happy Feet". It can be a really hard habit to break, and, at times, flat-out dangerous. I had explained to Reggie several times that walking away from your foe is really not the preferred method. Face the fish, get the rod up high and strip like there's no tomorrow; that's the technique, especially when standing in heavy current adjacent an angler-swallowing hydraulic. There's your top tip of the day, folks. And now, out in the very middle of a river flowing at 4500cfs, in really swift current, with a crazy, swirling drop-off a couple feet away, it was of the utmost import to stand in one place when setting the hook and fighting a fish. These were elements that I really made an effort to instill. Even as I buddy-waded him down to the money spot, I repeated the imperative. Can any of you guess where this is heading?

I think we fooled around six fish down there and had many other grabs or false grabs. Every stinkin' time Reggie went to move backwards. And every stinkin' time I reminded him not to do that. I'm not saying he was dense; just extraordinarily hard headed. Each time I would grab the strap on his waders to keep him from falling. After a while I just kept my hand hovering out in that vicinity, ready for the save. Eventually Steve hooked a really big fish maybe a hundred feet away from Reggie and I. There was no way of knowing what it was, but I knew that he'd never land it by himself without a net. So reluctantly I left Reggie and charged up through the heavy current to Steve. Right when I got to him, I looked down to see Reggie set up on a nice fish. In my mind I'm thinking, *don't move! Just keep your feet planted!* The first couple seconds, he was good. Then inexplicably he went to walk backwards. And then it happened. The river simply took his feet out from under him. He stumbled, this big, strong Jersey guy, and fell in. I've never run in a river. It's just not advisable nor necessary. But I ran to Reggie, who was, by kicking his feet at the cobbles, maintaining his position. And in this situation alacrity was of the essence. I did get there in time to help him to his feet before he slid over the drop. Incredibly two things happened right then... one, he was utterly unfazed at my mixture of concern and frustration, and two, the fish was still on! He continued to play the big Redband into the net while Steve was having a battle for the ages up-bar. We landed Reggie's fish, released it and then he was instructed to get back to boat and keep Patty company. I was giving him a good old-fashioned "time out". This one would be extended.

Back to Steve and his fish. He had hooked a decent steelhead. On a 4wt. And was now trying to drag the fish up over the ledge into calf-deep, heavy water. Just wasn't gonna happen. I tried several times to get him to come downstream a little, to be nearer the fish and the drop-off. This was one of those times that I just knew we weren't going to land the fish the way it was set up. Until you can lead a fish one way or the other and at least try lifting its head every now and then, you're just spitting in the wind; the fish has all the good cards. But Steve was determined to work the fish the way he was. I'll admit to loving the battle, the man vs. nature aspect. Steve was leaning back hard, testing the knots, giving it everything he had. But this movie only had the one ending, predictable as a Hollywood Rom-Com. That's Romantic Comedy to those who don't keep up on such things, and I certainly hope you don't. And just as predetermined as disturbingly attractive movie stars kissing into a filtered sunset as music swells and credits roll, this stout, sea-run rainbow eventually broke off Steve's rig and swam away.

We took that as a sign that it was time for the three-minute row to the house. It should be noted that Patty did not fish the last stop. I was so busy taking care of Reggie that I hadn't really thought to gauge her attitude, which I was soon to understand was not good. Another of their friends came down while I was getting out of my waders and told me that she was still bent at having been "yelled" at. Now, in my defense, *I* never yelled, and she *was* screwing up a really good fish. It warranted a certain decibel alteration. But I never yelled. I haven't yelled at another human in a long time. I was informed that she just needed some time and that she'd be fine. I felt terrible though. I would never do anything intentionally to bum out a client. No matter how hard I ride someone, it's always coming from a place of love and a steely desire to get him or her into fish. In Patty's case, it was too early in the day and she hadn't the time to get to know me yet; to know that no matter how, em, straightforward I can be at times, all I want is for my clients to catch some fish and have some fun. I hadn't gotten to know *her* either. Perhaps I would have learned that she is super sensitive and didn't really care about the fishing. Maybe I'd have just left her alone... Probably not. Just not my style. You're in my boat, we're catching fish. Simple as that.

By the time we are all getting ready to eat, Patty seemed like she'd gotten over her discomfort with me. We had some wine and appetizers, some laughter, some stories from the day. Several times I praised all three who had been in my boat on some nice angling. They had all caught fish, something that can't be said for a lot of people on that river.

That night I was treated like a king by my incredible hosts. There was seasoned lamb shank, grilled slowly with the most epic mint reduction glaze, fresh-picked broccoli, scalloped potatoes, more really good red wine than we could all drink, and company I'd keep over any dinner table, anytime, anywhere. Afterwards when all but Steve and I had taken to their beds, there was fine scotch on the deck overlooking the river as she sung softly. Late into the night he and I talked about, well damn, I can't even remember. But I do recall much laughter, philosophical thought, deep appreciation of life, stories of fish and where and how they were encountered. Then there was sleep.

In the morning, as my clients slept, I snuck down to the river and swung up a truly massive steelhead. This fish brawled for a solid ten minutes, rolling, running, diving. It was easily one of the bigger fish I've tangled with on the Deschutes. In the end, and just as Steve was wandering across the dew-covered grass, coffee mug cupped under his nose, the fish gave a big head shake and tossed the hook. Simple as that; as if I were merely a slight annoyance in the hazy dawn.

After breakfast three folks climbed into my boat just as the river raised 500cfs! I mean, you could actually see it happening. I gulped nervously but failed to mention this latest event to my eager clients, who, it should be noted, included Patty. I was a bit surprise, as the previous night she had begged out of a second day with me. I told she and the others that I'd love to have her in the boat again, but if she'd rather hang out at the house, I would completely understand.

Unsurprisingly, the fishing pretty much sucked all the way through lunch. We worked hard at it, but the fish were in "Caution Mode". Let me explain, or better yet, let someone more deep-thinking than I do it: Many years ago while working another large tailwater, a renowned local guide and (therefore) intellectual man once explained how substantial flow changes might affect the fish and fishing for them. It will help, whilst reading this next bit, if you conjured your best trailer park accent, or "Dubya", the Bush number forty-three, as it should be noted this occurred in Redding, CA. And it went something like this:

"Alright, lemme 'splain somethin' to ya, Griff. Hey, what the hell kinda name is Griff anyway? Sounds foreign. You a foreigner? Don't talk like one. But hell, where was I? Yea, so it's like this: Now I want you to imagine yer sittin' in yer livin' room and yer watchin' a game. Prolly soccer, cuz yer some kinda foreigner. Anyhoo, yer watchin' soccer, which you prolly call football, but whatever, and yer diggin' into a big ol' plate of chicken wings. God, I love wings. You love wings, Griff? Hell, I don't even care. And you prolly got a rack o' PBR tallboys just sittin' on the table next to the wings. Sheeeyat, that sounds like some kinda night don't it, Griff. Anyhoo, so yer five, maybe six wings deep, chuggin' on a brew and suddenly BAM yer livin' room starts shrinkin'. Walls, ceiling, everything's closin' in on ya. The light starts changing angles comin' through the windows. Everything you've gotten used to starts changin'. You might even have to get off the couch and on the floor cuz the ceiling feels so close to yer head. Yer pretty sure yer not gonna die, but damn shit just got REAL! So you duck yerself down next to the couch and wait for a while. At some point you realize the room's not shrinkin' anymore. Takes a minute or two just to sort that out. Then you look over and, whadaya know, the game's still on! So ya think, *Hells bells I ain't dead!* Then you take a little while to assess the situation. You know, like *Okay, I'm cool. Game's on. House ain't shrinking anymore. This spot on the floor's actually workable. I can see the TV and everything.* But let's be real here, Griff. It's gonna be a few minutes 'fore you start thinkin' 'bout diggin' back into those wings. RIGHT?!!! Even though they're still sittin' right in front of ya! Prolly all piping hot and smellin' like that chipotle barbeque sauce you can get by the gallon at Costco! O, you'll get back after 'em 'ventually, maybe even with a bit more vigor. How you like that, me usin' a big word like 'vigor'? Didn't think a hick like me had that kinda game, did ya? Anyway, yer gonna eat cuz you have to. But it might be a bit. Kinda depends on how much yer living room just shrunk. Or EXPANDED!!! Yea, dammit, goes both ways! Let THAT sink in for a minute! Yup, that just happened. Blew yer mind! Didn't see that one comin', did ya? That's why I call it **The** **E**xpanding and **S**hrinking Living Room Theory **A**s **P**ertaining to **T**rout **A**nd **S**almonids, or TESL TAP TAS, 'cept that almost sounds foreign. And I don't much like foreign stuff cuz it's weird and, you know, foreign. Anyhoo, that's my theory."

In all honesty, and I've really no reason to offer anything but, I might have embellished there just a touch. But that is certainly the gist of it. I refer to such soliloquies as *Sagacious Homies In Trailers*, or... you get the idea.

So on this day we experienced first hand and up-close the expanding living room theory. Aside from the obviously apparent changes in depth and weight, the subtle color and velocity alterations were there too. It was, by most accounts, a new river.

After lunch I put us on some water that felt as "normal" as any I could find, slightly re-worked their rigs, and split the three up. This spot had been really productive on recent trips so even with the bulging river I had a good feeling. Steve went upstream of a tree overhanging Patty and I. Reggie went a ways downstream and began stripping ridiculous amounts of line of his reel. I'd already learned that he wasn't into the whole *let's make some shorter, better presentation* thing. Nope, that was for sissies, and people who like to catch fish. Reggie was all about working great gobs of line way out there where the fish *weren't*, out beyond where they *were*; making one hideous drift after another. But far be it for me to remind him yet again where he should put his rig. You know, I'm just the guide. Nobody's telling Reg how to do anything. Not in this life. Hell, I probably wouldn't listen to me either. Dirt bag fishing guide. At fifty! How good could I be? What a waste!

Please don't get the wrong impression here. I really liked Reggie. I'd fish him every day of the week. He's super awesome, a really funny guy. And I'm not just saying this because he could probably pick the phone up and have me offed any time he felt compelled. You know, just the faintest gesticulation over an espresso at one of Steve's coffee joints in Jersey could put a whole series of events into motion wherein I get a knock at my door and some guy's there with a baseball bat, under orders to bust my kneecaps up a little. Not saying Reggie is that kind of a guy. But he could be. Probably is. Who knows? Anyway, I really liked him. A lot.

Where was I?

Oh yea, so Patty hooked four fish on successive casts fifteen feet in front of where we stood. One was a steelhead. One was a grotesquely obese 18" Redband. Suddenly, as if we'd walked over the searing coals, weathered hellacious storms and battled seething demons, Valhalla welcomed us, the weary, scarred warriors we were. The sun shone. The wind sang harmony with river. Patty laughed and giggled. She and I bonded. My heart sighed.

Her last fish took us on a solid downriver trek with Steve in tow. He had come around the corner to see what all the commotion was about. Reggie was wading back up through the riffle because I'd told him that the next fish would be his. Patty, Steve and I waded down past him, me holding her by the back of her warders. Little if any instruction was required. She now understood, best as any of us ever will, the *dance*. I just kept reminding her that I had a good grip and wasn't going to let her fall. We finished well down river, a gorgeous Redband folded heavily into my net. It was the perfect way to wrap up a couple incredible days. We did fish the guys up in the honey hole for a bit. Reggie got a nice one. Steve fooled a few but didn't land any. The three of them stood in the October sunshine giving each other shit, drinking beer and playing like children.

We rowed out slowly. No rush. The afternoon was as peaceful and beautiful as they come down there. They all fished the island above the ramp while I put *Ruby* away. Several times during that process I stopped and sat for a moment, head buried in hands, vaguely shaking in disbelief at the twenty-four-plus hours we'd shared. And also at the life I'm now living that brings people like Steve into it. He is a guy I can truly call a friend after the times we've spent together; and to steal his phrase "I'm a better Indian for it!" And did I mention that I really liked his friend, Reggie?

Next came a series of camp trips. The first was with two wonderful, hilarious and fishy gals, Kim and Heather. The famous Kevin would be the gear guy. Just the four of us for three days from Trout Creek down to Maupin. Kim, who you may remember from an earlier story, is pretty experienced and was looking to expand on techniques for fooling trout and steelhead. Heather, brand new to fly fishing, was just into having a bent rod in her hand. We had beautiful weather, perfect campsites, a relatively uncrowded river and plenty of fishing action. After a couple months working the "Day Stretch" pretty hard it was refreshing to be down there amongst the seclusion and beauty. There is a wildness to that 34 miles of river you don't get much in life. No cars, no cell phones. Very little to interrupt the grandeur. The first day we fished hard in the South Junction area, mostly with single-hand rods using a variety of nymph rigs; much of the same stuff I've been using upriver recently, along with a few bigger flies meant to attract steelhead. Heather got her first fish on a fly rod waist-deep in a really good riffle. Being alongside someone for that moment is always a rush and Heather made it all the more fun by being completely, unabashedly stoked. It would prove to be the first of many gorgeous trout she'd land over the next three days. Kim was putting in time, fooling a bunch of nice trout but really wanting to make contact with a migrating fish. She'd have to wait a bit longer for that.

Camp that night was full of laughter, tequila, music, good food, all the stuff riverside life should have. Dinner was pork loin marinated in ginger, garlic, shallots and soy sauce, then glazed with sesame oil, brown sugar and honey. The sides were pine nut couscous and curry broccoli. Dessert was gourmet chocolates. And some really good tequila! Then it was time spent around the campfire, singing songs, telling stories, being silly. This was one of those trips when you get the feeling real friendships were forged under a canopy of stars with the river humming softly out there in the dark. We were, though, at Whisky Dick so there would be no late night revelry. Whitehorse Rapid lurked just down river. We'd have to row her in the morning; not something that should be attempted while hungover or sleep deprived.

The morning dawned still and clear. We had a simple breakfast of fruit, granola, yogurt, juice and coffee. The plan was to break down camp and get downriver a bit. We'd spend the early part of the day targeting some prime steelhead water. As we worked on camp, Kim asked if she should fish. I told her that I highly recommend fishing, especially if you want to catch fish. That's why I get paid the big bucks. She wandered just upriver with my 8wt single-hander. Another guide service had sent their bagger, Matt, down there early and he was waiting just around the corner for us to clear out. Kim went in his direction. Not fifteen minutes later he came rushing into camp and told me that my client has a big fish on. We grabbed the net and ran back up to find Kim indeed tied to a steelhead. For those of you who haven't ever tangled with one of these fish or watched as someone else does, it really is a major event. Every steelhead -similar to trout- has a different M.O. and learning to predict its next move is critical to landing one. Kim was doing a great job with this fish. Her only issue was the shallow rocky bottom she was on extended quite a ways out and the river beyond was swift. Each time the fish was coaxed near enough to net, its belly would scrape the bottom and it would bolt for the middle of the river and then downstream again. My new best friend, Matt, was in the river holding my steelhead net. I was, it should be noted, and I write this with some shame, still in my "civvies" and camp boots. So it was up to Matt to land the fish unless we dragged it onto the shallow cobble, which is never my preferred method. So back and forth they went, this steelhead and Kim. Heather was down there watching too. Neither of the gals was familiar with the tenacity and strength of these fish. Fortunately Kim had great instincts for the give and take; the fine balance between dominance and submission. There is no rushing things with these fish, and that can be the hardest part for the uninitiated. As the fight wore on, there was little need to coach Kim. She was doing everything as it should be done. The fish was tiring. Matt was ready with the net. It was just a matter of time. And sure as anything we know of, the great fish eventually folded exhausted into the net after perhaps ten long minutes. It was a moment of quiet triumph, as is often the case with a big sea-run fish. There is a part of us that wants the fish to win the fight, a nagging desire to torment it no further. And so a collective sigh emits out into the ancient canyon, a release of thanks, apologies, respect. There were the obligatory photos of fish and angler, and then the slow walk back to camp.

We were packed and afloat by nine and on our way to the rapid. It was decided that we'd run without scouting as long as there were no signs above telling to do otherwise. The drift down was not rushed. Is it ever? A great golden eagle was flushed off a gravel bar mid-meal. A baldy with a four-foot wingspan ushered our way down river. The sun shone in a cobalt sky. And yet, even as the river ghosted along, we knew, at least Kevin and I, what lay beyond the next couple bends. The gals remained blithely unaware of the violent torrent we were approaching. At one point they were ordered to put on life jackets. A minute or two later they were asked to not talk again until told they could. Kevin, the far more experienced oarsman, led the way. I found my seam, rested, tried to slow the heart rate. Kept the boat at a comfortable angle. The sound filled first my right ear and then every sense I possess. Then a couple positive oar strokes over the "Knuckles", looking for "Hogsback" over my right shoulder, but all I saw was explosions of whitewater. I searched a split second too long. By the time my attention was drawn to what lay just ahead, "Can Opener" was right there! Luckily the two oar strokes I needed dug in and the boat pulled nicely off the nastiness. Unluckily, I was now reversing when I should have been spinning the transom from right to left. I remember distinctly beseeching of Ruby to back up into the eddy behind "Can Opener" while pulling with the right oar and pushing the left. My beautiful old boat spun on a dime and backed up perfectly. It took perhaps three strokes more than normal to hold her off the "Boulder Garden" on the right side, but she went where instructed and posthaste we were scampering headlong into the chaos that is the "Washing Machine". For some reason -perhaps because the river already knew I'd pooped my waders- the waves parted perfectly and we got through taking on minimal water. Then there emitted the completely involuntary war hoop into the canyon walls.

In the small cove behind "House Rock" we pulled the boats in. I grabbed a beer from the cooler and jumped onto the bank where I sat on a rock facing the river. The only time I ever drink a beer while guiding is right there, having navigated Whitehorse, with the rest of my life laid out before me, my heart overflowing with love of the river goddess, my veins pulsing pure adrenalin. Most of the beer goes in the river as a gesture of gratitude and an invocation that the river continues to humor my presence.

The rest of the day was relatively uneventful. We did not touch another steelhead as the sun shone bright and the air warmed to a comfortable low 70's. As pleasant as the weather was, you want it a bit nastier for the steelheading to be really good. There was little complaining as the afternoon descended on the canyon. Kim caught several more beautiful Redbands. We arrived at camp for appetizers and cocktails. Dinner was New York steaks, spuds and Caesar Salad. We ate heartily under the stars with a small fire burning nearby. A more enjoyable evening is hard to imagine. And by the night's end we all wished there was one more to look forward to.

In the morning, after fishing camp water hard to no avail, we ate breakfast burritos with melon, coffee and juice. Then we broke camp and made our way down the last ten miles of river. The highlight of the third day was Kim hooking into another tremendous fish as a light rain fell. This was a brief encounter. The big fish ran her out to some heavy current, gave a couple big head shakes and broke off the whole rig. There wasn't much that could be done in this case. Sometimes those fish just own the situation. We re-rigged and got into some really nice trout before moving on. Both gals ended up having a fun day as the weather lifted and closed in throughout. We had several seasons in one day. But by the take-out we all agreed that the drift had been both a successful fishing trip and about as much fun as could be expected, or handled.

There was one day to turn around and take four guys form Toyota down the Warm Springs-Trout Creek stretch for a fairly unusual two-day camp trip. Because one of them couldn't stick around for both days, we camped at Trout Creek instead of along the "Day Stretch". These were guys from over in Portland as well as here in Bend. There was a mixture of experience. A couple of the guys were set on swinging with two-handed rods while the others were fairly new to fly fishing and wanted simply to get a fish on. They went with me. The swingers jumped in Martin's boat. These are the days we guides dream about; gorgeous weather, we were in no rush, and all we had to do was fish to Trout Creek and set up camp. At our first stop of the day we were into fish right away. My guys, Ben and Rob, both got with the program right off the bat and were making great presentations and hooking fish. Maybe an hour into the day Rob, who still hadn't landed one, hooked a gigantic steelhead. We were using stout 6wt rods with a combination of flies on tippet anywhere from 2-4X. Not being sure which fly the fish had eaten we were reluctant to try horsing it in. As it was, we really didn't have that much say in the matter anyway. When this fish made its move towards the Columbia, that is where we went. Ben had reeled in and was wading with us. At one point we got up on the bank to give chase. From up there I got my first proper look at this steelhead. It was one of those 9-10lbs fish that we just don't see that often. Maybe it was the same one that shook me in front of Luelling a week earlier! We followed this fish way down river. Rob did brilliantly. There's really nothing I would have done different. He kept great pressure, let the fish run, worked the rod at various angles, all that stuff. At least a quarter mile downstream and ten minutes into the fight I finally thought that maybe we were actually gonna land this thing. I was thirty feet below Rob. Ben had my camera at the ready. The fish was beginning to poop out. The stars were aligning. And then... Anyone wanna guess what happened next? For those of you who thought that the fish rubbed its belly on the bottom, exploded for the middle of the river and broke off the entire rig, well aren't you the smart ones. Yep, after all that. The fish simply had massive reserves. I can't remember feeling so gutted at the loss of a fish. Rob was stunned. Having never played a fish on a fly rod for any period of time, he just figured that we had it; nothing could go wrong, which is a great attitude to play fish with, by the way. Most of us would have known how many ways that battle could end in the fish's favor and played it with way more stress. But Rob was just dancing with no preconception as to all the potential pratfalls.

It was a long walk back up the bank, the three of us talking the whole way. Rob was equally stoked and confused. I tried to explain that the line we were using did have a breaking strength and sometimes these fish can easily exceed it. I told him he'd done incredibly well, all things considered. I told him in complete honesty that I wasn't sure I could have done any better. I told him repeatedly that we'd get another chance soon.

Back up at our run I re-rigged both guys, got Ben into a good spot, and positioned Rob a little lower than where he'd hooked the steelhead. His first cast went unmolested. But his second one... our collective world exploded anew. This fish was not nearly as large as the previous one, but easily twice as indignant. We briefly had hope that it might stick around our run. Nope. In that proverbial blink of an eye, the focus of our every attention was tearing out towards the middle of the river, extracting line from the reel at a heady pace. There were several spectacular mid-river jumps, impressive runs, insane subsurface rolls and cartwheels. I will spare all the details, until we ended up way down river...again. From the moment he hooked up, Rob handled this fish with the touch of an angler. A little ways below where we'd lost the last steelhead we came across some guys fishing. Turned out to be a couple buddies, one of whom, Matt, guides down there, the other, Jacob, is a client at our shop. They were cool enough to reel up and let us play the fish through their water. As much as I'd wish we'd stayed clear of them, we just weren't in control. This fish was leading the way. The struggle continued for another minute or two until the fish tired enough so we could get its head up and then slide it's hefty body into the net. All this time, from the moment we fooled it, I figured we had a steelhead on. It's that time of the year. The fish had fought with all the brute strength and tenacity of one. But once this fish was folded into my net and I got a good look at it, I realized it was a great big trout! We all four came in and hovered over the net, bumping heads to get a close look. Yep, a trout. Those of us who spend a bunch of time down there know how rare this fish is. We marveled at the size and beauty of it. A truly extraordinary fish for the Lower Deschutes. We got a handful of pictures before releasing it. And then this fish lay calm, exhausted in my hands for a solid minute before kicking back to life and vanishing.

The big trout proved a hard act to follow. The rest of the day offered up a bunch of nice trout but no more steelhead, at least none that we can confirm. We did get broken off a couple times by large, unseen foes. I can report there was much fun had in both boats all the way to Trout Creek. Once there we set the boys loose on camp water. As is usual around the ramp this time of the year, there were a bunch of buddies around and we all shared stories from the day over a beer or two. I just loved not having to rush out; nowhere to be, no one looking for me.

Eventually Martin and I got back to work setting up a comfy camp. We got some appetizers served, a nice fire going and prepped a big steak dinner for the boys. I'd like to inform that the night went without incident, but that would be a big, fat lie. Yes, sadly this night would end with a filleted phalange. The only good news -for everyone else- is that it was my finger that encountered one of Martin's really sharp knifes; not one of theirs. We did our best to clean and dress the wound but it was bleeding pretty badly and undoubtedly not very sanitized. Martin and I persevered and finished cooking. Dinner was served and eaten. The fire crackled flames into the night. The boys all enjoyed beers and laughter. Sadly, Rob had to get back to Bend, so he split after dinner. A while later, once the other three guys hit their tents, Martin and I stayed up late reflecting on what a cool season we've had and all that there is to look forward to. We spoke reverently of the Lower Deschutes; it's history and heritage. His understanding and knowledge of the great river's legend is impressive. This was the first time he and I had the chance to hang like that. Made me like the kid even more. At twenty-six he is on his first full year of guiding the Lower D. It's been rewarding and fun to oversee his growth as a young man down there. So even as much as my finger hurt and I was a pooped pup, we stayed there by the fire for a little extra while sharing stories. Sometimes in those moments I have to pinch myself that I'm on the job; that I spend time like that as part of my living.

In the morning my finger throbbed intensely and was incredibly sensitive to touch. I got up and started coffee. As Martin and I began prepping breakfast, I silently evaluated the day ahead.

Knot tying would be difficult at best. Rowing and making lunch and handling the boat at the ramps was all doable, with some discomfort. Not to mention how detrimental a prolonged infection would be to the last busy month of my season. We only had the three guys, so in theory I could fish one guy, or Martin could take all of them. I stole a look at the finger and didn't like what I saw. It was just a mess, obviously not as clean as it ought to be and maybe requiring a stitch or two. So after a brief talk, Martin and I agreed that he would take the remaining three guys for the day and I would get back to town for treatment. This proved a good idea.

We made breakfast for the boys, got their gear organized and stowed and then they left for the ramp and another day on the river. As soon as they drove off, I was overcome with remorse for not going too! I've prided myself on answering the call. This season had already seen me on the sidelines once. And it's important to me that I don't feel and act like the old man of the river, even if I am. But on this day, given the circumstances, I do feel like the right decision was made.

After the boys drove off, I took my time breaking down camp, packed all the gear in the truck and made my way up the road from Trout Creek at a very unfamiliar hour.

I was in town by noon and had the finger checked out. A nice woman at the BMC Urgent Care took a look and decided that even if the cut had required stitches originally, it was now simply a matter of cleaning and sealing the wound with skin tape. She did seem to take perhaps too much pleasure in proving how dirty the wound still was as she held it open and poured solution over it. "Irrigation" it's called.

Sadistic freak. I was given a small container of skin tape and sent on my way. And yes, I know you're all on the edge of your seat now, positively wracked with curiosity as to how my finger has healed. Quite well, thank you.

Just for the record, one of Martin's guys stuck a big steelhead that day as the crew floated Warm Springs to Trout Creek again. Damon had put in the necessary hours dedicated to swinging up some steel. We are always extra happy for the angler committed to catching a fish on the swing and Damon certainly understood his odds weren't great, but he stayed focused and was properly rewarded. Getting one swinging on the "Day Stretch" is always reason for celebration. Congrats, Damon. And Martin too.

A few days later we welcomed a crew to town for yet another overnight trip. For this one we'd set up a smaller camp at one of the flats along the "Day Stretch". There were four clients in two boats. Sterling would be joining this trip as fellow guide. The leader of this group was the incredibly dedicated and increasingly fishy Nandra, a woman from Jacksonville, Florida, I had out for an overnighter earlier this season. It would appear I've created a monster in this one. She is completely addicted, reading fly-fishing literature, practicing her cast, focusing laser-like on her next chance to catch a trout. She brought three of her colleagues along for an awesome couple days in the canyon. In my boat was Nandra and a work associate from Portland, Brenda a complete newbie. I had been looking forward to fishing Nandra ever since she booked the trip and had heard Brenda would be a quick and eager study, so as we pushed off the ramp Saturday morning there was much reason for hope. As it turned out both gals got quickly into fish. Nandra's first trout was a beautiful slab. Brenda played three or four fish before we got one in the net. There were several hook-ups that might have been steelhead. With these nymph rigs I've been employing you really just never know.

We enjoyed a mellow day taking our time from spot to spot and having the luxury of really giving each stop a thorough seeing to. We pulled into camp that afternoon and got the folks situated in their tents, then fished camp water prior to dinner. Nandra, unsurprisingly, fished the hardest and hooked the most fish. This lady is just unstoppable! She fished right till dark just above camp as the sunset lit the canyon sky in pastels. I poked my head around the corner to check in on her sporadically as we made dinner, taking special reward in watching one of my protégées clamping on so completely to fly fishing. She was just happy and content to still be knee-deep in the great river, working on tension and roll casts and a variety of mending techniques we've dialed in together. Such focus and intent on improving at any style of angling is gratifying to behold.

Sterling and I prepared a massive steak dinner for our clients that we ate out under a calm, starlit sky. The evening was incredibly comfortable for late-October. Then the moon, still waxing, crept over the eastern rim of the canyon, lighting up the western wall, then across the river until our camp was aglow. We had a big fire going in the saucer, more good wine, stories and laughter galore. This night only ended when the wood ran out. If we had brought more, we all may have stayed up till dawn!

In the morning, after a hearty breakfast, we set the clients lose on camp water. Some swung while others kept at it under bobbers. Some just sat back, drank coffee and enjoyed the beautiful new day. Once the boats were packed, we set off in search of fishy water. The river was quite busy that whole weekend and Sunday proved a challenge finding good water even though we had gotten out in front of most day drifters. At our second stop we hit pay dirt and stayed in one zone for the next few hours, only moving up or down bank every now and then. The old saying "You don't leave fish to find fish" was especially relevant that day. We only pulled anchor when it was time to make for the ramp. Some days are like that down there, either because of how busy the river is or just finding a spot with lots of feeding fish. That day was a bit of both. But I'm not sure we would have pulled anchor regardless of the crowds. The fishing was that good.

By early afternoon the trip did have to come to an end and so we rowed for Trout Creek under a heavy, damp, "steelheady" sky. Saying goodbye to those folks was hard. I'm sure we will see some of them again, but until then we'll miss their spirit and ability to really, fully and completely enjoy the majestic canyon.

The very next day found me back down there with two of my favorite clients, Pat and Larry. They are retirees in the area, having moved from Texas some years ago. He is just flat-out skilled and she is one of the most gifted beginners I've ever had the pleasure to guide and teach. But what makes guiding this couple so good for me is their appreciation of the river, the canyon, the day away from electronics, cars and people. Each time we slide under the bridge at Warm Springs I can feel their enthusiasm and love for the place emerge. And each time we get rigs in the river they catch fish! Pat has become easily one of my fishiest clients. Everything I tell her to do, she does. She never over complicates situations. She knows what a good drift looks like. And she can SET THAT HOOK!!! Everywhere we stopped that day fish were caught. We certainly targeted steelhead in places, but the trout fishing was so danged fun it was hard to pass up.

At our second to last stop I had a season highlight when I was mid-riffle landing a really nice Redband for Larry when Pat yelled down that she had one on. I could see her line, tight and racing for the middle of the river just as one of my not-so-favorite guides down there came around the corner, two clients doing impressive statue impressions in the front of his boat. He trying to not to look our way, but the look on his clients' faces was priceless. Please don't get me wrong; I really hope they caught fish too. Really. I do.

Or maybe I don't.

Either way it was pretty funny. The moral of the story is if you want to have fun like the Pat and Larry, you gotta be in my boat. Or Martin's. You know, one that says "Fly and Field Outfitters" on the side.

As we rowed for the take-out I let the boat glide for periods, oar handles beneath my knees, not in any rush to have the day end, knowing that Pat and Larry were luxuriating in the slanting, autumnal light. Knowing it would be the last time I would see them this season gave me a heavy heart, but also reason for massive gratitude that the universe saw to it that our paths crossed in this life. Until next season, I will look forward to fishing those two over and over again.

With the 10th month winding down, I had a trip with a local doc, Bill. He is a long-time angler and customer at the shop who I've had the pleasure of guiding once before out on the Crooked River. He's got plenty of game and an eagerness to get better still. We were armed with both single-hand and Spey rods for a day of properly probing all the money spots for trout and steelhead. It is a rare treat to have a solo angler in the boat. I can really focus on every aspect of their presentations and they get their ass fished off! We fished every good spot all day long with perhaps a little more emphasis on the single-hand stuff. What I'll remember most from our day together, aside from what great company Bill is and what a dynamic, multi-faceted life he lives, is that I'm not sure I've ever seen so many fish hooked but not landed in one day by one person! And this is for a guy who can fish! It was just crazy how many different ways the fight ended in the fish's favor. After a while losing fish almost became expected. And through all of it, Bill kept his cool, stayed positive and focused, and kept fishing. Lesser men would have caved. I know because I've seen it. You ever play golf with someone who actually has a good swing, a nice consistent move, who you just know is capable of making pars, but on *that* day he has a hard time hitting it out of his shadow? Apart from hoping he hits it well because you don't have a black enough heart to enjoy his flailing (or do you? Maybe there's some money riding on it) you're also not sure how he'll react if he keeps shanking everything. Clubs might start flying. Profanities of all color could be screamed at uncaring divots, execrations towards humanity in general can sail downwind where other groups of golfers cower. Well, the same moments can occasionally exist on the river, when some poor soul feels the stars have momentarily misaligned for them, that God in all her wisdom has seen fit to torture, to test the spirit, to find out what someone is made of; if, at their very core, they possess the temerity to continue. I'm not exaggerating here! These moments actually occur! Well, I'm pleased and unsurprised to relate that Bill would be undeterred, would remain positive and full of appreciation for his position in the grandest scheme of things; the mettle of a man truly displayed. And behind him a guide stands on the bank, smiling.

Oh, fish were caught. Don't get the wrong impression entirely. But the redside population as a whole scored a resounding victory on the day. Right up until last light, the 10th hour of fishing, the 10th mile of our float, late in the 10th month of the year, Bill kept at it. We found a little bucket not far from the ramp where I believe we hooked ten fish. A couple of these were genuinely large trout in full ass-kicking mode. Bill fooled and danced with some amazing fish. He didn't get broken off once! I think we landed one... And yet the equable spirit of the man endured. It's rare I'm left completely speechless, without words of either encouragement or condolence. But in this case I found myself capable only of shrugging shoulders, and little else. My mind raced through other flies we could use with bigger hooks, different water where the angler might begin the battle from a slightly more advantageous position, some equation that might end up with a fish folded into my net. But Bill was determined, serene even. I got the sense that all was right in his world, that our lack of words was allowing a closeness to an energy that only he felt right then, right there.

And now that I think back on it, I felt something too as I stood high above the run watching. Lacking any form of conventional creed, I'm not sure if there's a way to explain. But you know me; I'll try anything once. In that soft, cooling evening, as Bill fished golden-hued water, my boat bobbing nearby, a hackle-soft breeze whispering through the canyon, with each trout hooked and lost, I felt the cycle of birth, life, death; samsara, as Buddhist's refer to it. I saw forests burn and re-grow, listened to rivers flood and abate. I felt centuries of Native American's footsteps, countless generations, newborns, warriors and elders. In this cyclone of silent energy there was a celebration, great ceremonious bonfires blazed, the season transitioning as the earth spun on axis, infinitely against an endless blanket of galaxies.

Then Bill's bobber dove for the bottom of the river.

Chapter 16

Whisper Me To Sleep

How many nights, my love, have I lie astride you just like this? Here, under the interminable ceiling of cosmos, where I'm made to feel so tiny and magnificent at the same time, your sweet song cradling me. Through a narrow slat between hoodie and sleeping bag I watch shooting stars and satellites sing through the sky. The Milky Way washes from one canyon rim to the other. Here, yet again, in my whisky-soaked and weed-stained pre-slumber I feel embraced without judgment of past sins or trepidation for future shortcomings. And as visions of your surface exploding with violet trout fill the space between consciousness and chaos I ask only one more thing of you: Whisper me to sleep now, my darling.

Chapter 17

The Pilgrimage to
Where She Awaits

March

I saw the most beautiful sunset the other night. It was similar to so many we get treated to in Central Oregon this time of the year; all streaking pastels over jagged ten thousand-foot, snow-covered volcanoes; all transient explosions amidst color gradient perfection. What made this one especially cool was that I was "watching" it in my side view mirrors, driving east on 20, Pilot Butte bacon cheeseburger and onion rings causing threatening rumbles. Minutes earlier I had kissed wife and daughter goodbye, filled the gas tank and begun the four-hour drive east. This is where she awaited me. Every year I leave it all and run to her. This has become something of a pilgrimage for me. Each year, after the Sportsmen's Shows and still feeling a little soiled, I unplug, disconnect, grab a bamboo fly rod, fill the cooler with beer, the dog jumps in the back seat and we go. Where? Well, some of you may already know; I'm heading east from Bend and it's March. I'm sure some of you can guess. Many will recognize the canyon or the fish. This is not a secret river. I'm still not naming it. She's not mine to covet, but she and I have our own special thing for sure.

The drive was mellow. There's a new speed limit out there, recently raised from fifty-five to sixty-five, but for the most part I stroked it at around seventy miles per hour, listened to music and eased myself into the idea of no cell phones, no computers, no talking, and no one to discuss plans with. This time is precious to me. In my life as a year-'round guide and instructor this is the mellow period; the calm before the storm.

The concept of an annual pilgrimage is not new to me. Back in California, for a couple decades there was an autumn trip to Trout Country every year, no matter what. The trip was always taken solo. It was my time to romance and seduce my mistresses one last time before the snows and cold of winter sheltered them from me, and me from them. Sometimes I just went to the McCloud for a few days; sometimes I'd sweep from the Upper Sacramento to the McCloud and then on to the Pit River and Hat Creek depending on weather and fishing conditions, sampling what each had to offer. There were years when I'd get a hotel room in Mt Shasta and wander mile after mile of the Upper Sac in snowfall and massive Blue-Winged Olive hatches. Those trips were my time to ease out of trout season, say my "good-byes" and wander back into some semblance of "normalcy" that waited in the low lands, amongst all the decay that had overcome my childhood dreams. I'd write in journals, read, sing to campfires, drink tequila and beer, smoke some grass, fish and sleep. Not always in that order. I'd gather and organize months worth of fishing notes, plot trips for the next season, process the meaning of *my* life amongst the chaotic cosmos. But mostly I'd fish my ass off, dawn to dusk, just me and Satchel, the lab. And in my most private moments I would bow, hands pressed to heart and give all my thanks for another incredible chapter.

And so now I've begun a new ritual of anti-social self-indulgent trout bum disappearance. And as the Eastern Oregon night engulfed me I felt free, Eddy the Aussie, perched on the center console staring off into the headlamp glow.

At some point early on I realized I'd left my reading material -the latest Vanity Fair as well as David James Duncan's classic *My Story As Told By Water*, constituted the only literary fodder for this pilgrimage- on the arm of the sofa. I planned on doing a bunch of editing of my second book, tentatively titled "Fool You Once, Shame on Me...", so it wasn't as if I needed something to read; just something well-written. At some point, still a little ways west of Burns, I acknowledged that only having my own writing to keep me company out there for three days might provoke lunacy. So once in town I pulled into the Safeway and went shopping. Now were I a gun fanatic, I'd have had literally dozens of quality magazines to choose from. Or if off-roading was my thing, boy could I have gotten my hands on a bunch of good stuff. As it was, and after several minutes of standing statue-like, I grabbed a Maxim and the latest Rolling Stone tribute to David Bowie. The Maxim, if anything like it used to be, would prove entertaining on some entirely base level. It promised an article about Steph Curry, a baller we been loving for way longer than his mega-star days, and a story about the Virgin Islands, a land I once called home, and some pretty pictures of, you know, stuff. The Rolling Stone, well that was just to make me look like something other than a complete pervert. *And* I'm a Bowie fan.

Back on the road, the 5-Hour Energy doing its dirty work, the stereo up a notch or two, the blackest night you can imagine. Freedom personified. Into her embrace I flowed.

The throat of her canyon greeted me around 10:30. In the absolute dark I stumbled around till I found my favorite campsite.

Getting the tent set up went quickly. Within minutes the Aero Bed was inflated, my Kelty bag was laid out with an old comforter over it, a pillow placed just so. I've gotten quite good at this "roughing it" thing. This was going to be the best night's sleep ever so still and quiet it was. The river through there is defined by long stretches of barely moving water. I was camped on one of these, with the slightest riffle hum just upriver. But there was much bird song, distant coyotes, and the occasional sound of a large trout attacking a hapless mouse. I heard the otter that lives across the pool come over to tear a branch from the willows near my tent. And then sleep overtook me.

For about one hour.

I awoke to find the Aerobed had gone utterly flat. The dog didn't seem to mind as she spooned me. But the cobble rock was now molding into my back in a way that was painful and no doubt causing subluxations. I figured I must have not sealed the vent cap and so took a minute to open and re-lock it. Out into the frigid night in only underwear and Ugg boots -now there's your mental picture- to start the truck and activate the pump. Once accomplished it was back into the comfy bed for sheer delirium.

For about one hour.

This would prove to be a long night. Much as I'd love to report that I slept through one of these painful alarms, this story must be factually correct and to that end I will dutifully relate that almost exactly every hour I was rousted and made to get out of the tent to fire up the truck and pump the mattress. I did try to pad the area and sleep through it, but the tent was in a really bad spot.

Daylight came around 5:30 and I was up and out. Coffee was made. A bamboo rod strung up, waders donned. A brand new day. Sleep? Who needs sleep? Out on the river there was no activity. I'd expect some midges to start coming off soon and trout to begin feeding, some sign that she felt me at her side.

Then I saw the first rise. The fish, a brown trout pushing eighteen inches, was in maybe ten inches of water, occupying a narrow seam, no more than three feet off the river's edge. Eddy and I went into tiptoe mode. This is what we came for. This would be three days of fishing with no split shot, no bobbers, no sinking lines or heavy flies. And let's go back to that cane rod for a second. If any of you suffered through my first book, the literary equivalent of waterboarding, and cryptically titled "Middle Fork", you were properly introduced to this lovely stick in the "Happy Valley with Scott" chapter. Yes, the Jim Hidy built, hollow-core, eight-foot five-weight named, ingeniously, *Heidi.* This is a rod I've had for over twenty years now. These days it doesn't get much use, sadly. So much of my life is spent in a drift boat with clients, no place for a rod such as this. So she comes out once in awhile on the Fall or Crooked. One of these days she'll make an appearance on the Lower Deschutes. But out there, amidst my mid-winter lust, way beyond my "normal" life she gets to play. And then I suppose we should revisit the quarry. This river is home to a truly astonishing number of brown trout. Twenty-five years ago an ODFW biologist with an affinity for browns saw to it to plant a few truck loads of them, regardless of the reality that the river in question held a genetically pure strain of redbands. But, oh well, boys will be boys, and the result is a fishery that boggles the mind. As much as I adore Redbands -and if anyone were to see fit to "contaminate" a native strain nowadays, I'd see to it that they suffered intensely in one way or another- the ensuing growth and proliferation of browns out there is mega. So you have this little river, full of big brown trout eating mostly tiny bugs on or near the surface. Oh, how my demented mind warps; my decades long perversion for this situation can finally be fed. My desperate, groping need has found its soul mate.

So that morning I tied on the size twenty Sparkle Dun with a size twenty-two CDC Midge a couple feet behind and began casting. The presentation was made difficult by many factors, not least of which I was crouching fifteen feet from the river's edge. The fly line and most of the leader would be landing on parched river rock. A three-foot drift would be considered a success. These are the situations I crave; such is my tweaked version of romance. This first fish of the day would not be fooled. I was able to get a dozen or so casts over it before it slid out into the riffle and hid behind a rock. This is a scenario that plays itself out repeatedly there. Oh, there are easier fish to fool. Lots of 'em. And there are more rudimentary tactics to apply, sure. But I'm there for the challenge of a big fish on a tiny dry; much else doesn't interest me. I've caught browns there on mouse patterns and leeches; actually had a carp eat a little leech last year. But the amount of quality fish eating dry flies through the day is what I make the trip for. And I'm just fine with not fooling one, because there's a good chance another fish is working very nearby, and out there I'm happy to play the numbers game.

And so on the third or fourth fish I went after I got to watch it tip up and to the side just a little as it ate the midge. Now for those of you who don't know me very well, that is the instant that still makes me get all giggly as an angler. Much as I love a grab on a swung fly, or watching a bobber dive for the bottom after a glorious, complicated drift, or a Chubby Chernobyl vanish in a torpedo attack, the fish holding in shallow water moving casually to eat a size twenty fly is *the* thing for me. As this fish ate, I stood up and set the tiny hook and all hell broke loose. The wild thing was to see how many fish spooked out when this one began thrashing. I hadn't even seen them until they all bolted in different directions. And these are large fish in super skinny water, blending in magically. The browns out there this time of the year tend to be a bit snaky and don't fight with a ton of vigor, which is just as well; sixteen to twenty-inch fish on little dries fished off 6X tippet is hard enough without getting broken off all the time. The winters are tough for the big fish with no bugs of substance in their food chain. The pool fish are usually chunkier, but most times getting them to eat requires stripping leeches, which we've now come to understand I am at loathe to do there. So it's the tight, technical riffle water I prefer. Getting an adequate presentation takes every bit of what mediocre skill I possess, making the reward of fooling one all the greater.

That morning maybe a half-dozen really beautiful fish were fooled before I drove upriver to a spot we call *The Aquarium*.

Unsurprisingly, there were already a couple guys up there, fish rising everywhere and a whole lot of head scratching going on. A nice, older guy walked down the far bank, across maybe seventy-five feet of silent river. He sat on his bank and me on mine. We ended up chatting for a solid half hour about the river. I didn't get his name but he used to live in Bend and now calls La Grande home where he owns a sporting good store. He had great stories about fishing around Bend in the 60's and 70's. I'd never heard about the Rotenone dumped in the Fall River years ago to try eradicating the brook trout. He also told me that ODFW plants rainbow trout in the river right where we were chatting. I was under the impression that no fish were stocked out there anymore. I can only imagine how the big browns must enjoy those days with a bunch of hatchery dummies swimming straight into their toothy mouths.

Eventually the guys bailed from *The Aquarium* so I went up and began fishing. This spot is so named because you can see the fish clearly as they fin in a fairly narrow channel no more than three feet deep. I love to just stand and watch them eat. Most times you can easily see fifteen to twenty fish within a short cast. The thing is that these fish are probably the most attended to on the entire river during low-flows and so are the hardest to fool. The Blue-Winged Olive was just beginning to come off. There were still a bunch of midges around too. So I put a Baetis Hackle Stacker on the end of fourteen feet of leader and tippet with a Biot Midge behind it. The first grab was a cool one to watch. The fish twitched when it saw the dry and then as soon as the midge nymph came into view he just crushed it. This was another sixteen-inch beauty, all heavy headshakes and short, thrusting runs. I netted it and then giggled softly at how ridiculous the tiny fly looked in its gnarly mouth. I suppose it's no wonder the fish are a bit skinny this time of year; such little bites. Maybe I should try that diet.

At some point I was shaken out of my fishing reverie by the reality that I had to figure out some solution to my mattress situation. On the drive back down to camp there were run after run full of trout eating Blue-Winged Olives. The river right in front of camp was boiling with rising fish so I caught a handful and then attended to the previously mentioned issue. I diagnosed that the problem was the cap wasn't sealing and so found some duct tape in the back of the truck and set about attempting a patch. No matter the method of tape application the air still leaked out if even the slightest weight was put on the mattress. Eventually I just taped over the entire opening wherein the cap sits. I did find another small leak in the actual bladder and taped over that too. After filling with air I put the mattress back in the tent and lay down. A couple hours later I awoke to find some air still held. I'd napped into the evening. A quick inspection of camp water showed no fish rising, so it was campfire time.

After a dinner of big steak and some fire-baked spuds it was back into the tent and out of the elements. The wind blew rain sideways much of the night. My mattress patch job held as well as could be expected offering a few good hours of shut-eye at a time. I'd have slept better but for the wind. This trip was turning into a sleep-deprivation experiment. She had beckoned only to torture.

I was up again at first light, groggily making coffee, stumbling with a distinct lack of clear thought and balance. Coffee helped. So did the pack of donettes. I read an interview with Bowie's from the mid-70's, a time during which he did massive amounts of cocaine and babbled on as if a man possessed by Kerouac, on blow. Hilarious stuff. Then I edited one of my stories for a bit, had a second cup of coffee and began feeling it.

That morning was spent at a couple pools above camp before heading to *The Aquarium* where I was planning on meeting a guy I know well from the shop, Brian. Two things of note occurred that morning once at *The Aquarium*. One, a couple old dudes waded in below me, where the river loses almost all momentum and behaves more as a pond. They began making long, elegant cast and then slowly retrieving some kind of offering. And they started catching fish. Lots of 'em. I mean like tons of fish. Double after double, hootin' and cacklin' away like drunks. I'll come back to these old fellas in a minute.

I was having fun doing my obsessive dry fly thing over several feeding fish. But my browns were in an especially antisocial mood as I tried a half-dozen flies to no avail. The morning was overcast, warm and without wind. It wasn't until I put a size twenty-two Tailwater Tiny a foot off the Miracle Midge that I got a grab. Just as I was releasing this fish, Brian, and his friend from PDX, Steve, walked down. We exchanged pleasantries while I changed to a different fly combination. I pointed out all the fish right out in front of us including one brown that is the most vibrant gold color. I call it *The Albino*. It sticks out dramatically in the run where most fish blend in. I told those guys I've watched that fish eat a hundred times, put dozens of flies over and passed it. It's never eaten my fly. Every time it eats a natural I find myself swearing at it and calling it really unkind and unnecessary names. Which brings us to Number Two. While those guys rigged up I flicked my latest offering out. I now had on a size twenty Sparkle Dun with the size twenty-two CDC Midge behind it. Yup, two tiny dries. Super perv, huh? This is what she does to me, how she possesses my imagination and will. On the second cast *The Albino* turned and came for a look. Then kept coming, all the way to the midge, eating it in one of the more visually badass grabs I can ever remember. I announced to the guys that I'd got him. Brian took some pictures as I played and landed the fish, which was, like most, a little skinny, not as big as I'd made him out to be, but extraordinarily beautiful. A nice, hearty swig of Scotch followed. Yea, it was only nine in the morning. So what?

Later I ventured upriver and found more nice fish in a big, shallow pool. After fooling a couple and spooking many more, one really big brown made off with both dries after easily busting the knot. The same two flies went back on, but the action tapered off. At another pool, with at least ten fish working, I only hooked one and it shook me pretty quickly.

Back down at *The Aquarium*, Brian and Steve had left. The old guys were still downriver crushing. The wind began to blow a bit.

I put the Biot Midge off the back of the Sparkle Dun and began casting. On maybe the fifth cast I set the hook at some movement below the dry fly. What happened next is still a little hard for me to believe. The water right in front of where I stood erupted as a rainbow in the seventeen-inch range went completely ballistic. This brawl was way more intense than anything a brown trout is capable of there. Two long runs, each followed by awesome jumps, heavy surface thrashing. The bamboo was utterly in its element now, bending from the cork, protecting the fine tippet, allowing the fish it's time to exhibit just how displeased it was. The old CFO reel, long since possessing a functioning drag system, zipped with each burst and emanated warmth after the second run. It would take several minutes before this fish succumbed to my net. After removing the miniscule fly from its jaw I actually posed this fish for a palm shot, something I rarely do anymore. It wasn't a huge fish, just such an anomaly for me out there.

The guys downriver had taken to their truck by the time I released the fish. I was ready to head towards camp, maybe fish down there or grab a beer and snack. So Eddy and I got in the truck to go. I had to pass the guys on my way out so I stopped and asked if they were leeching and if so, what kind? You never know how such questions will be received streamside. But as one of them came towards me, the other hopped out of the rig, and before answering the question, said, "Dang, that looked like a good rainbow you just got."

"Yea, for sure the best one I've ever had here," I said, scrolling through my phone for the picture. They both leaned in.

"Oh, heck yea! Lookie here," one said to the other. "That's a fatty!"

"Oh yea!" the other replied to one. And then to me, "Nice 'bow there, fella."

I liked these guys right away. They end up telling me about some of the truly massive browns they'd caught out there. One of the guys told me he was eighty and had fished the river for seventy-five years! I did get privy to their technique of the day. Good news is that I know it works. Bad news is that I had very, very few similar flies to those they showed me. They were *not* leeching. We ended up B.S.ing there for ten minutes. They loved talking about the different ways they fish the river. Supposedly, up to a couple days previous, the fish had been on something completely different. But the old boys knew what was up and made a stunningly effective technique change. Those fishy old dudes, with their neoprene waders, baloney sandwiches and big fish stories made my day. And they conferred on the spot that recently they'd hooked, played, seen and almost landed a ten-pound brown right down there. More than once.

On the drive back to camp I passed miles of fishy water, most of it with trout rising. Once there, I grabbed the rod, a cold beer and headed down to the riffle. Sure enough fish were rising everywhere. Well, maybe not everywhere, but if I scanned one hundred and eighty degrees from down river to up I could see twenty to thirty fish eating within a thirty-five foot cast. The winds had died, there was one guy fishing way down the pool. Game on.

The first cast was accosted. The second mauled. The third annihilated. Each fish was in the fifteen to seventeen-inch class. I honestly can't tell you how many fish were fooled over the next fifteen to twenty minutes. It was as chaotic as any flurry of dry fly I've had in a long time. Then Brian and Steve got there and the fish stopped eating. Seriously, it was pretty bazaar. I may have been releasing a fish when they showed up, or had just put one back, but I remember thinking that it's gonna be cool to take turns with the bamboo, each hook a few fish and then take a break. But the fish just stopped eating. And didn't really start again. Oh, how this fickle lass taunts.

That night was unremarkable. A big fire blazed, some BBQ chicken and couscous went down nicely, I finished the Bowie stories, edited for a bit and then slept. The mattress was much the same as the night before. A proper night's sleep would evade me out there.

After breaking down camp in the morning I made my way to a pool upriver and rigged for the technique the old guys had employed. At least until the real hatch began, this would be a fun experiment and as much as it went against the dead-drifting of little flies on or near the surface, it was done with flies every bit as small, if not smaller! Indeed the very smallest flies I possessed were put into action. Not long after starting, the first fish ate one. This would prove to be the smallest fish of the trip, a foot-long rainbow, but fought with determination. A while later while lost in thought I felt sudden tension in my line. My first impression was that I'd hung up on something. Then that something moved. It didn't offer any animation, just movement. I raised *Heidi* above my head and stripped a few feet of line. Then I saw it. Like a serpent it ghosted towards the surface, still offering only weight. This was an enormous, dark trout no more than forty feet out, facing upriver, not struggling in the least. I'm going to tell you the truth about what happens next even though the recollection causes a quickening of my pulse and it would appear a slightly more enthusiastic tapping of the keyboard. I panicked. Instead of calmly putting a bit more pressure on the fish in hopes of burying into its jaw whichever tiny hook it had eaten, I yanked hard... hard enough to simply extract said hook from said jaw. In that moment the fish made for the bottom leaving a swirl that consumed the entire center of the river. Now, I'll admit to the occasional exaggeration when it comes to fish size. I don't carry a tape measure and so what might have been a thirteen-inch fish quite easily becomes "fourteen to fifteen". Over the years, if anything, I've taken to under-guessing. But I think with most fish around a foot I can be pretty accurate. So this thing, this beast, this Loch Ness Monster I'd just encountered, well I'm just gonna state here and now that it was well over two-feet long and would have weighed eight pounds, at least. And screw you if you don't believe me. It is the second such fish in that size range I've seen with my own two bloodshot eyes on that river. They're there. I'll get one next time.

That's really where this story could end. But it won't; not just yet. I will tell you that the old guy's technique worked beautifully. The day promised good hatch conditions right up until the wind began blowing. I fished with Brian and the boys for a while. And then I began the homeward migration, fishing here and there on my way out. A fish or two was fooled. Mostly I just wasn't in a big rush to reenter the world of cell phones, work, chores and schedules. The world of mattresses that don't leak did have a certain appeal though.

Outside Burns I was humming along when I saw a Statey parked on the other side of the road. I looked at the speedo and was a couple clicks over seventy. Didn't think much of it till he pulled out behind me, tracked me down and began his own little private Fourth of July. Damn, those guys really like all their flashing lights, don't they. I pulled to the side and switched off. He approached. "Hi there. My name is State Trooper Rodney," I'm not shitting you here. That's how they introduce themselves.

"Good evening, State Trooper Rodney," seemed the polite response.

"Just want to let you know that we're being recorded here," he announced, as cheery as you can imagine. Eddy panted "hello". "Do you know why I pulled you over this evening?"

"Not really sure," I lied.

"Had you going eighty back there. That's pretty fast."

Against all my overwhelming desire to profess there and then that if in fact I had been going eighty, I'd still have had another forty or fifty in me before what I'd consider 'pretty fast' on that particular ten-mile straightaway, that 'pretty fast' held entirely varied definitions in this world, I offered only, "Well I don't recall going that fast, State Trooper Rodney. And if you knew how terrible the gas mileage is in this thing at *seventy*, you'd know that I'd never intentionally go *eighty*."

He requested and made off with license, registration and proof of insurance. Minutes later he returned, handed me my things and wished me safe travels. Yup, let off with a warning. Me! Can you imagine? That only ever happened to me once, and I had to scour my deteriorating memory to recall the event. I'd just gotten my license, pulled over for a "California Stop" -that's where you don't completely stop at a Stop Sign- and was let off with a caution. Oh man, if that little Mill Valley piggy knew what was in the back seat that night...we'd have all been in the papers, but that it's for another story. This one now must mercifully end.

Thanks for coming along. Until the next time, perhaps you should make a pilgrimage of your own. Visit a special love. Fall into her welcoming embrace. Allow yourself that decadence, that moment of reverie, that time when your hearts find a similar beat and your keel feels weighted enough for you to navigate the rest of the world's storms. She out there, waiting. Pay her the time.

Just sayin'.

Peace and love till the next time.

Acknowledgements

and Apologies

Well, here we are again, at the end of another book, and so now it's time to give the thanks and praises to those who are deserving. It is also when I feel compelled to offer humble apologies to the many people in my sphere who live in this life with me, those who see little of me for great swathes of the year while I traipse from one river to the next, from one *other* to another.

Firstly, dear reader, I'd like to thank *you*. As any passionate writer would profess, the craft itself is done from a very selfish place. *I* write because I need release, I crave this cathartic process through which my life occasionally finds a modicum of balance. A sad reality is that the creative mind finds very little peace in this world. When I'm writing I find mine. But the other undeniable element that led to compiling these stories is that I love the thought of entertaining people. It's been that way for me since my very first performance playing music at the tender age of thirteen. While the applause is sweet, the *connection* is what matters, what turns me on. And so now this is my way to connect. My sincerest hope is that some part of this book entertained on something other than the basest level, that there was a resonance in a sentence, paragraph or page, and that it spoke to a part of you the rest of the world knows not how to communicate with.

I have to give acknowledgement and apology to my amazing wife, Michelie and our beautiful daughter, Lola. It is these two who have suffered my absence the deepest over the years since we moved to

Oregon. As much as we needed the change in our environment, and we've landed in a great place, in no way could Michelie have predicted what our life would morph into here. I do my best to give them what I can when I can, but there are extended periods of the year when we see very little of each other. And yet somehow they are always here when I get home. Even as I wake up most nights mid-nightmare that a different situation awaits after yet another three-day camp trip on the Deschutes. In that R.E.M. sphere, I arrive in our driveway with drift boat in tow, the garage door opens to reveal an empty space where the Subaru is normally found. I go into the house and find nobody home, not even the dog. There's a note on the kitchen counter relating that they've had enough, they're heading back to California and I can come visit anytime I like. In this dream, while my heart races and weeps, I possess a complete and utter understanding as to why they've left. There is not a trace of anger, only a supine acceptance that they did what they had to do, and that I'd probably have done the same. But they don't leave, or at least haven't yet. They stay against all better reasoning. And I could hardly be more grateful. They are my keel. My compass. And the reason I strive to be a better man everyday. Michelie is my best friend and soul mate. Lola is the coolest little human I know. And so to them, I say "thanks" and "sorry" yet again.

To the rest of my family I must also give massive thanks. They've been through so much with me, all the changes, life's many paths and alternates routes. I've made some pretty whacky decisions and they've stayed with me, supportive and encouraging. So to my mom and stepdad, my sister and brothers, step siblings, in-laws, all the nieces and nephews I can't thank you enough for being such a diverse, interesting bunch. I miss you all. Please come visit.

To my first wife, Theresa, the mother of Jasper, my favorite human; she is the best person I've ever known and one of my dearest friends, I can't thank her enough for everything she's been to me and everything she's done for our boy. It is because of her that he is the most extraordinary young man. Every wonderful quality he possesses comes from Theresa, except good balance, that one he gets from me. And now as he embarks on an angler's life, I offer additional thanks that she is so cool with letting him do what his heart tells him. The "Marshall Three" lives on even as we've taken our own paths, and that warms this old, weary heart everyday it continues to beat.

And Jasper, oh up-and-coming fishy one, I couldn't be more grateful for the young man he's become. Through all of it, he's stood by me, and I him. I've never been more proud of another person. I've never felt judged or misunderstood by this old-soul. And watching him grow up into the compassionate, tolerant, funny guy that he is fills me up with hope for the next generation.

Once again I have to thank my old fishing buddy, Stefano for all he's been to me in my life as an angler and as a man. He was there early on, the only person in my circle of family and friends who *attempted* to understand what this fly fishing thing meant to me. He came along on trips to be a supportive and interested friend, sitting alongside rivers and on the shores of lakes, writing poetry, making campfires and mixing cocktails. He did eventually get himself a fly rod and make himself into an angler as well. Then we were an unstoppable force, exploring blue ribbons on any map we could find, in search of fish but also looking for the intangibles. We knew that there was more to us than who we were in the lowlands. And we were convinced that we could find that part of us in the mountains, wading rivers with rods in our hands, challenging everything we thought we understood, never knowing exactly what lay around the next corner. And to this day, when I'm walking the banks of a river, he's there, egging me on, an enduring energy.

All the sages must be mentioned. From Dan Gracia who managed the only fly shop in San Francisco way back in the day, and humored my incessant questioning; to Jim Pettis for being the best guide and angler I've ever known, who was patient yet demanding of me during our many days together, for pushing me to get better and not letting me become complacent, ever; to Jack Trout for giving me my first guiding experience and the chance to discover how much I loved it, for exposing me to Chile, for helping unlock many of the McCloud River's secrets, I'll always be grateful for our time together; Jim Hidy, the master rod builder who has been in my life for twenty years, his eight-foot five-weight is the finest wand ever built, but more importantly, his friendship, eager ear and amazing storytelling voice are all things that have enlivened my path as an angler; and finally to all the nameless characters I've encountered along river banks over the last thirty years, I've learned so much, shared beers, smokes and stories with countless people, young and old, women and men, beginners to experts, each meeting was important and impactful, and I try to pass along a little of each of you to every random person I come in contact with.

And now here in Bend, Oregon I've been so blessed to meet and fish and work with so many incredible people. There is no order that makes sense to me in mentioning these folks, so it'll just happen randomly: My boss (how random is that?) Scott Cook took me on as an unknown entity a little over three years ago, and our relationship has taken on shapes and forms neither of us could have imagined, as we now manage what is the coolest fly-fishing company I've ever known, growing a business, working our asses off, becoming good friends and feeling nothing but positivity regarding the future, and I can never thank him enough for the opportunity he's given me; our buddy and fellow manager at Fly and Field, Dave Merrick for being the humble sage presence he is in my life, staying calm when the world goes all ape-shit and sharing a wealth of knowledge while asking nothing in return, a more genuine and generous man I've never known; the whole crew I've shared these last three years working with, from those who have moved on to those recently joined, we are brothers who have been through the wars together, bonded by our love of what we do; Martin Csizek, the hardest working twenty-something I've ever known, an up-and-coming guide with more potential than any of us realize, and as motivated an angler as you'll ever meet, not to mention one of more interested and interesting men I've ever known; Travis Lucas for becoming a man I can truly refer to as a friend, someone, regardless of how different our upbringings were, I feel I can say anything to and he to me, not often in life I've felt that way, and his calm advice and quiet ear have been large for me; Chris Nolte for being my rowing coach, for letting me figure out how much I still had to learn and then teaching me, he was there for my first run through Whitehorse and not a pass through that rapid happens without his voice, a more wise and experienced river man you'll rarely meet; Neal Burrell, an amazing guide and inspiration to many of us with far less experience, a calm, professional energy we can all learn from; Sterling Dillingham, an incredibly dedicated and skilled angler at such a tender age, a talented musician, and someone, although nearly thirty-years my junior, I've "grown up" with around here; the co-workers Danny, Quintin, Russ, Gabe, Austin, Kyle, Lewis, Kevin, Lundberg, all guys I've been in the trenches with, we've gotten it done and I'm proud to call you all friends and co-workers; the rest of the fishy fuckers here in Bend: Curtis, Tim and Steve, Malanga, Nutter, Lenny, Kellan, the beautiful Celeste, everyone of them has shed energies into my world, all ya'll make me feel like the luckiest trout bum ever for having our paths cross.

And oh the clients, the varied, passionate souls who have seen me fit to spend a day with, whether working the banks of the Crooked or drifting the mighty Deschutes in *Ruby Redside*, so many incredible memories shared and created, so many puzzles solved, so many leaping trout, so much laughter and an appreciation for the hieroglyphic maze that is angling; my life would be a lesser experience were it not for you.

Tomorrow. I'm grateful for tomorrow. To continue parenting Jasper and Lola, the chance to make Michelie feel adored, wanted and treasured. I look forward to being a student and a mentor in the fly-fishing community. I can't wait to find out what's around the next corner in this life, and sharing that discovery with all those I love.

Until we meet again,
Griff